THE PRACTICAL GUIDE TO RAISED BED AND CONTAINER GARDENING

Easy-to-Follow Gardening Solutions to Grow Organic Vegetables, Flowers & Fruit in Any Space for a Bountiful and Year-Round Harvest

GG BARRE

Table of Contents

Hello Readers,

Thank you for purchasing my book! To show my appreciation, I am providing a FREE listing of **150 plant profiles** that can be downloaded by scanning the QR code below. Plant profiles provide more detailed information about specific plants, such as soil preferences, germination times, etc. This download includes the profiles provided at the end of this book in Chapter 6, and much more! This comprehensive listing includes Vegetables, Herbs, Flowers, and Fruit from all US states, including Alaska, Hawaii, and the territory of Puerto Rico.

Introduction

Welcome to a journey where tiny seeds and empty containers blossom into lush gardens brimming with life! Whether you are standing amid urban concrete or gazing out at a small yard, the joy of cultivating your own plants is within reach. I'm thrilled you're here, ready to turn what may seem like small, confined spaces into thriving gardens. I'm a gardener and nothing excites me more than sharing the magic of gardening. Over the years, my trowel and seeds have been my tools not just to cultivate plants but also to nurture well-being through all seasons.

This book is crafted with one goal in mind: to make gardening simple, enjoyable, and fruitful for everyone—no matter your experience level, physical abilities, or the size of your living space. Whether you've felt the sting of a plant wilting despite your best efforts or you're taking your first tentative steps into gardening, this guide is your companion.

But who am I, you wonder? I am the person who has killed nearly every houseplant I've ever owned and considered myself a black thumb. So why should you be taking advice from me? Because I went through the journey you are about to embark on and have been successful, which goes to show that if I can do it, anyone can! I was born and raised in Hawaii, and was unaware that plants were of annual or perennial variety. Where I grew up, everything pretty much grew whether you wanted it to or not. Since moving to the mainland, where I've now spent most of my life, I've <u>had</u> to learn a thing or two about completely different climates. Each year when spring arrives, I am amazed at how life returns so brightly and boldly, and I get caught up in the excitement!

So let's clear up a common gardening myth right from the start: "You need a large yard to garden successfully." This couldn't be farther from the truth! Raised bed and container gardening opens up a world of possibilities, allowing you to grow a vibrant garden on patios, balconies, and beyond—spaces you may have never imagined could support life.

Structured to walk you through every aspect of gardening, this book is divided into key sections:

- Foundations of Raised Bed and Container Gardening
- Essential Tools and Techniques
- Gardening Challenges
- Harvest
- Reflection and Looking Forward
- Plant Profiles
- Helpful Terms and Definitions

Not all sections may apply to everyone, and that's perfectly fine. Feel free to navigate to the parts that resonate most with your current needs. Some, or perhaps many, of the plants described here will not be familiar or will not grow in the region of North America where you reside, and that's okay too. To ensure we are all on the same page, I've included a section of common terms and definitions, since these were not so common to me and may not be to you either.

Each chapter unfolds in a clear, step-by-step manner, equipping you with everything you need to start and sustain your garden. From selecting the right tools to understanding the best plants for your climate, I'll be right here guiding you. By the end of this book, you'll not only have a garden but will have nurtured a new part of yourself—someone who connects with nature and enjoys the fruits (and vegetables!) of your labor.

So, grab your gardening gloves, open your heart and mind, and let's dig into the first chapter together. Your garden awaits, and I'm here to help every step of the way. Let's grow something beautiful together!

ONE

Foundations of Raised Bed and Container Gardening

D id you know that the most ancient gardens discovered were surrounded by walls or raised mounds? Even our ancestors knew the secret: a little elevation can transform gardening. In this chapter, we dive into the foundational knowledge of raised bed and container gardening. Whether you have sprawling outdoor space, just a few feet on a sunny balcony, or no outdoor space, these methods open up a world of possibilities. They're not just practical options but also vibrant solutions that add depth and beauty to your home.

Together, we'll explore how these structured spaces can help overcome common gardening challenges like poor soil and pest invasions, all while making your gardening efforts more manageable and rewarding. So, whether you're looking to spice up your culinary routine with fresh herbs just a few steps from your kitchen, or you want to cultivate a dazzling array of flowers, you'll find the insights here to start you on the right path.

1.1 What is Raised Bed and Container Gardening?

Raised Bed Gardening

Raised bed gardening involves cultivating plants in soil that has been elevated above ground level and is often enclosed by a frame made of wood, stone, or other materials. This method offers numerous advantages that make gardening more accessible and enjoyable. First, by raising the soil level, you enhance drainage, which is crucial for healthy plant growth. No more waterlogged roots or, conversely, soil too dry to sustain life!

There are essentially two types of "raised" beds. The first is simply a mound of soil that is flat on the top and that sits on top of the existing soil. To assist in containment, a frame is built as the sides of this flat mound. The other type of raised bed is one that actually has legs like a table and that suspends the soil in a container significantly higher than ground level.

A raised bed warms up quicker in the spring, extending your growing season. You can start planting earlier and keep going later into the fall than you would with a traditional garden. Another often-celebrated benefit is the ease of maintenance. With your garden raised above ground level, tasks such as weeding, watering, and harvesting become less strenuous. This is particularly beneficial if bending and kneeling are challenging for you. Plus, by controlling the soil in your raised beds, you can create the perfect mix for your plants, unaffected by the natural soil in your yard that might be less than ideal.

Raised beds also offer protection from some pests, such as slugs and snails, and make it easier to install barriers for others like rabbits...having the bed significantly above ground level becomes the barrier for some pests. The aesthetic appeal is a bonus as well! Raised beds can be designed as stunning visual elements that add structure and beauty to your garden.

Container Gardening

On the flip side, container gardening involves growing plants in any vessel suitable for holding soil, from traditional pots and planters to more creative containers like old barrels, buckets, or even repurposed furniture. Talk about a win-win situation! Repurposed or recycled containers can add texture and artistic flair in unexpected and delightful ways, keep more material out of landfills, and lower costs. Container gardening is incredibly versatile and can be adapted for indoor or outdoor spaces. It's an ideal solution for gardening enthusiasts who may not have access to a yard but still want the freshness of home-grown produce or the beauty of blooming flowers.

One of the primary advantages of container gardening is the control it offers over the growing environment. Each container can be customized with the perfect soil mix, improving plant health and reducing the risk of soil-borne diseases. Containers also reduce the risk of pest problems and make pest management more straightforward.

Additionally, containers can be moved to take advantage of the best weather conditions or to protect plants during extreme weather. This mobility makes it easier to manage light exposure, with the ability to shift plants to ideal locations as the seasons change. For those living in urban areas or with limited space, container gardening can transform a small balcony, patio, or even a windowsill into a lush, productive garden.

Whether you choose raised beds, containers, or a combination of both, these gardening methods offer flexibility, efficiency, and accessibility. They allow gardeners of all levels, especially beginners, to experience the joy and satisfaction of gardening without the need for extensive space or advanced skills. With these approaches, you can grow a variety of plants, from vegetables and herbs to flowers and fruit trees, adapting as your confidence and experience grow.

1.2 Raised Beds vs. Containers: How Do I Choose?

When you're standing in your potential garden space, whether it's a sunny patch of your backyard or a cozy balcony, the question often arises: should I go with raised beds or container gardening? Both methods have their unique set of benefits and limitations, and the right choice often depends on your specific gardening goals, physical conditions, and the space you have available. Let's explore these aspects to help you make an informed decision.

Benefits of Raised Beds

Raised beds are like mini plots that offer a neat, compact gardening space with enhanced soil conditions. One of the standout benefits of raised beds is their ability to improve soil conditions rapidly. Since you're filling the beds yourself, you can tailor the soil mixture to suit the specific needs of your plants. This is particularly advantageous if the native soil in your yard is rocky, nutrient-poor, or clay-heavy. By creating the ideal soil environment, you can boost plant health and increase yield.

Another significant advantage is the extension of the growing season. The soil in raised beds warms up more quickly in the spring and retains heat longer into the fall. This extended season allows you to plant earlier and harvest later, which is a great bonus if you're looking to maximize your garden's productivity. The raised nature of these beds also means you have to bend down less, making gardening more accessible if you have physical limitations or prefer not to bend or kneel.

Why Choose Containers

Container gardening, on the other hand, is the epitome of versatility and mobility. Containers can range from hanging baskets and traditional pots to more creative solutions as previously mentioned. This method is particularly suitable for urban gardeners who might only have small spaces such as balconies or rooftops. Containers make it possible to cultivate a garden in areas where traditional gardening is just not feasible.

The mobility of containers is a huge plus. You can move your plants to optimize their light exposure throughout the day or season, and you can bring delicate plants indoors during adverse weather conditions. Containers also allow for individualized soil treatment, much like raised beds, which can lead to healthier plants and better growth outcomes.

Limitations and Considerations

Both gardening methods come with their own set of limitations. Raised beds, for instance, can require a significant initial investment in materials and soil. They also demand a bit more labor upfront to build and fill. Once established, they are relatively permanent structures, which means you need to be confident about their placement in your garden space.

Container gardening, while versatile, can sometimes be limiting in terms of plant size and root growth, depending on the size of the containers used. Larger plants might not thrive in a restricted space. Additionally, containers require more frequent watering than in-ground plants or even raised beds, as the soil in containers tends to dry out faster.

Making the Right Choice

Deciding between raised beds and containers often comes down to evaluating your space, your physical condition, and your gardening ambitions. If you have a bit of yard space and are looking for a "semi-permanent" setup that could yield a substantial amount of produce, raised beds might be the way to go. Depending upon the material used to create your raised beds, they can typically be used year after year. They're excellent for growing everything from herbs and flowers to substantial crops like tomatoes and root vegetables.

If you're an apartment dweller with a sunny balcony or have limited outdoor space, containers could be your best bet. They offer enough flexibility to grow a variety of plants, from small vegetables and herbs to flowers and even some smaller fruit trees. Containers are also a good choice if you foresee the need to move your plants regularly or adjust their location seasonally.

Also consider that raised beds with or without legs can come in a variety of sizes and don't necessarily need to be a semi-permanent setup. They can be used on balconies, porches, or indoors as space permits.

In essence, both raised beds and containers offer unique benefits that can be tailored to suit various gardening needs and preferences. Whether you choose one or the other, or even a combination of both, you're taking a step towards creating a garden that suits your lifestyle, meets your food production or aesthetic desires, and brings you joy and fulfillment. As you set out to make your choice, consider the long-term commitment and upfront investment, and balance these against the benefits and yield you expect to gain from your gardening efforts. The best garden is the one that you enjoy tending to.

1.3 What Kind of Raised Bed Do I Want?

When it comes to choosing the right type of raised bed for your garden, think of it much as selecting a new piece of furniture for your home—it needs to be functional, fit your space perfectly, and hopefully, add a touch of beauty. The material you choose for your raised bed can have a substantial impact on its longevity, cost, and how it integrates with the environment of your garden. Let's explore some popular materials used in raised bed gardening, each with its unique properties and aesthetics.

Choosing the Material for Your Raised Bed

Wood is one of the most commonly used materials for raised beds due to its natural appearance and relative ease of use. Cedar and redwood are particularly popular choices because they are naturally rot-resistant and can withstand the elements without the need for chemical treatments. These woods provide a classic, rustic look that many gardeners appreciate. However, the cost can be higher compared to other woods, so it's worth considering your budget. On the other hand, treated lumber is less expensive and is treated to resist rot and pests, but it's preferable to use wood treated with natural, non-toxic substances to avoid any harmful chemicals leaching into your soil. Douglas fir can be purchased and hand-coated with natural linseed oil as a reasonably priced alternative.

Fabric is becoming more and more popular as these beds are lightweight, portable, and relatively inexpensive. The fabrics are durable and have excellent properties for drainage and aeration. In addition, because they come in a variety of shapes, they can be just what is needed for a small space. An added benefit is that they require no tools to assemble. With a choice of colors, they can give your garden a fun, smart look.

Galvanized steel is another excellent option, especially if you're going for a more modern look. It's incredibly durable and resistant to corrosion, which means it can last many years without any need for maintenance. The metallic finish can add a contemporary edge to your garden, and the material does a good job of keeping the soil warm, promoting early spring growth. However, it can be more expensive initially and might not blend as naturally into every garden setting.

Recycled materials such as old bricks, concrete blocks, or even repurposed wood can be cost-effective and environmentally friendly options. These materials can add a lot of character and make your garden bed into a conversation piece. Using recycled materials saves money, helps reduce waste, and aligns your gardening practice with eco-friendly principles. Keep in mind though that depending on the materials, longevity and pest resistance can vary.

Visualizing Raised Bed Materials

Each material lends a different aesthetic and functional edge to your raised beds. Imagine a wooden cedar bed as a warm, earth-toned frame that naturally ages into a soft gray, blending beautifully with green foliage and vibrant flowers. In contrast, a galvanized steel bed might shine under the sunlight, its sleek edges offering a neat contrast to the organic shapes of plant leaves, fitting perfectly into a minimalist or industrial-chic garden design.

Figure 1 Wood frame, galvanized steel, fabric, and recycled brick raised beds

For those who like DIY projects, constructing a raised bed from wood pallets can be both a budget-friendly and creatively fulfilling endeavor (I'll show you how later in **Section 1.5 How Do I Build a Raised Bed?**). Truly, a variety of recycled materials can be used and even used together. They can be painted or decorated to match your personal style, making your garden truly one of a kind!

Where to Purchase Raised Beds

If building a raised bed from scratch seems daunting, there are plenty of pre-made options available that can save time and effort. Many garden centers and online retailers offer a wide range of raised beds in various materials and sizes. Prices can vary widely depending on the size and material, but generally, you can expect to spend anywhere from $20 for a 6 ft x 3 ft rectangle fabric bed, $50 for a simple small wooden bed to several hundred dollars for larger, more durable options such as those made from galvanized steel.

When choosing where to buy, consider the quality of materials used, the reputation of the manufacturer, and the design options available. Many kits come with all the necessary components and can be assembled with minimal tools and effort, making them a great choice for beginners. Additionally, shopping locally can be beneficial—you can often get good advice and insights from local experts who understand your area's specific gardening challenges.

Selecting the right raised bed for your garden is a balance of functionality, budget, and personal preference. Whether you opt for the warmth of wood, the versatility of fabric, the durability of steel, or the sustainability of recycled materials, ensure that your choice supports the overall health of your plants and fits harmoniously with the aesthetic of your garden space. By choosing wisely, you'll create a solid foundation that supports your gardening endeavors for seasons to come.

1.4 What Kind of Container(s) Should I Choose?

Choosing the right containers for your garden is much like picking out pots for your favorite houseplants—each option offers a unique style and set of benefits, and the best choice depends largely on your individual needs and aesthetic preferences. Just as in the world of fashion where the material of your outfit can make a big difference in look and comfort, the material of your containers significantly impacts the health of your plants and the overall look of your garden.

Let's start with the basics. Containers come in a variety of materials, each with its own set of advantages and considerations.

- **Ceramic pots** are quite popular due to their aesthetic appeal and substantial weight, which make them stable and suitable for larger plants. However, they can be fragile and heavy to move, and they often require more frequent watering due to their porous nature
- **Plastic containers** are lightweight, affordable, and retain moisture well, making them a great choice for gardeners who are just starting out. They also come in an array of designs and colors, allowing for personalized garden aesthetics. On the downside, they can become brittle over time if exposed to too much sunlight. Consider this, especially if you live in a climate where it's sunny/warm most of the year.

As a kid, oftentimes when I picked up a plastic container from the side, right above the soil line, the container would inevitably crack from the weight of the plant and the brittleness of the plastic. For this reason, concrete pots are used fairly often in Hawaii, but these can become quite heavy depending upon their size and what's placed in them. For this reason, they are commonly filled with orchids growing on hāpu'u (tree fern), which thankfully makes for a light load.

- **Wooden containers** bring a natural and rustic look to your garden. They are more durable than ceramic and naturally insulate the soil, helping to regulate temperature. Cedar and redwood are particularly resistant to rot and pests. However, wood can be susceptible to weathering and may require occasional treatment or replacement.
- **Fabric pots**, a newer option, have gained popularity for their breathability, which promotes healthy root growth and prevents overwatering issues. They are also lightweight and easy to store during the off-season but can deteriorate faster than other materials.
- **Recycled materials:** For those with an eco-friendly bent or who love DIY projects, they offer a unique and sustainable option. Old barrels, buckets, and even kitchen colanders can be transformed into attractive planting containers. These choices reduce waste and add a distinct character to your garden. Just ensure they have adequate drainage and are safe for growing food if you're planting edibles.

When deciding on the size of your containers, think about the mature size of the plants you wish to grow. Larger plants like tomatoes or small trees will need more root space, so opt for bigger pots that can accommodate growth without tipping over. Smaller, shallow-rooted plants or herbs are fine in smaller pots. Always consider the space you have available—larger containers can crowd a small balcony but might be perfect on a spacious patio. Remember, more soil in a larger container holds moisture longer, so if you can't water often, bigger might be better.

Be creativity in your garden! This can transform it from a simple collection of plants into a reflection of your personal style. Consider painting clay pots to match your outdoor furniture, or decorating plastic containers with mosaic tiles. Even something as simple as coordinating the colors of your containers can have a dramatic effect on the overall look of your garden. If you're crafty, you might enjoy turning old items into planters. An old boot, a discarded bicycle basket, or even a child's toy truck can become a quirky and charming home for your plants. Skies the limit—pop a plant in that chipped teapot you don't know what to do with but can't seem to part with. Or place several plants in a stone fountain that no longer works—and just see what it does to enhance your space.

Choosing containers for your garden is an exciting opportunity to blend functionality with style. By considering the pros and cons of each material and matching the size of the container to the needs of your plants, you can create a thriving garden that is as unique as you are. Whether you opt for the natural elegance of wood, the vibrant versatility of plastic, or the sustainable creativity of recycled materials, your container garden is bound to be a source of happiness and pride.

1.5 How Do I Build a Raised Bed?

Building a raised bed for your garden can be a deeply satisfying project. It's crafting a miniature sanctuary where your plants will thrive. The process is straightforward, but the impact is significant—providing a healthy and controlled environment for your plants to flourish. Constructing a raised bed is a practical step towards a more fruitful gardening experience. Let's walk through the materials you'll need, considerations for design, and step-by-step instructions to build your raised bed, including an eco-friendly option using recycled materials.

List of Materials and Equipment Needed

To start building your raised bed, you will need some basic materials and tools. The items can vary slightly depending on the material you choose for the bed (e.g., wood, metal), but here's a general list to get you started:

- **Building material:** Wood (e.g., fir, cedar or redwood), galvanized steel, or any recycled material such as untreated wooden pallets.
- **Fasteners:** Screws (stainless steel or coated for outdoor use) for wood; bolts and nuts for metal.
- **Drill:** For making pilot holes and for drilling in

screws (if using wood) or **Wrench** for tightening nuts (if using metal).

- **Saw:** If you are cutting wood or any material to size.
- **Tape measure:** To ensure correct dimensions.
- **Staple gun and landscaping fabric (optional):** To line the bottom of the bed, controlling weeds and providing a clean base, if desired.
- **Level:** To make sure your bed sits evenly on the ground.
- **Hammer or rubber mallet:** Useful for assembling parts without causing damage.
- **Gloves and goggles; optional face mask:** For personal protection during cutting and assembling.
- **Optional linseed oil and brush:** To protect frame if using untreated wood (fir, for example).

Height and Depth and Accessibility Concerns

Choosing the right height and depth for your raised bed is crucial for both plant health and your comfort. Ideally, the height should be between 6 to 12 inches for most plants; however, if you plan to grow deep-rooting vegetables such as carrots or potatoes, consider a depth of at least 18 inches. Also consider if you are going to be using a bed that sits on top of already existing soil. If you are growing carrots or potatoes and the soil under your bed is adequate, you may be fine with a 12 inch bed (measured from ground level). Leave the bottom of the bed unlined and the longer roots will then be able to penetrate below the 12 in depth of your bed.

If you are using a raised bed on legs and want to grow plants with deep roots, filling to a depth of 18 inches may be your only option. A deeper bed depth (at least 12 in) may also be required if you plan to use teepee trellises that need their prongs sunk into the soil for security. Remember, the deeper the bed, the more soil you will need, and soil will be where you'll be spending a significant part of your budget.

The top 6 to 12 inches of the bed is where most plants will do most of their growing and so you'll need to fill your bed with at least 6 to 12 in of nutritious soil. If you need to fill your bed deeper than this, you can save some money (and weight) by using organic material that will eventually break down, such as branches, sticks, newspaper, straw, and pine cones. Don't use grass cuttings as these can become odiferous when wet and soggy.

If you have back issues or prefer not to bend down, using a raised bed on legs at a height of 24 to 30 inches is optimal, making gardening much more accessible. If you will be using multiple beds, don't make the mistake of not leaving enough room between beds. Make sure the paths between them are of sufficient space, especially if you are using a wheelbarrow, wheelchair, or any other equipment. Map out how much space you'll actually need to turn and maneuver easily. Ensure that the bed's height is comfortable, whether in a wheelchair or sitting in a chair.

Building My Raised Bed

Here's a step-by-step guide to building a raised bed from wood, one of the most common materials due to its natural look and affordability. Building one from other materials will be similar, although different tools may be required. For example, the type of saw for cutting wood will differ from a saw that requires a blade that can cut through metal versus wood. Fasteners such as nuts and bolts will need a wrench to tighten, etc.

If you are building a raised bed "in-place," (resting on top of existing soil and the frame may be too heavy or difficult to move once it's been built), read **Section 1.6 Where Do I Place My Raised Bed?** first to build your raised bed in the proper location.

1. Plan and cut your material: Based on your desired dimensions, cut your wood to length. If you are coating the wood with linseed oil or an equivalent, do this first and let dry prior to assembling your frame.

Say we'll be building a standard in-place 4x8 foot bed (largest recommended bed size) on existing soil. We want it to be 12 in deep and we want to use 4"x4" x 8 ft planks. Consider the type of plants you'll be growing in your bed to determine the appropriate width of your planks (which will then determine the depth of your bed; reference **Height and Depth and Accessibility Concerns** above). We'll need at least nine (9) planks and one (1) additional 4"x4" plank at least 48 in long.

- Three (3) 8-foot long planks stacked on each other for one long side of our rectangular frame
- Three (3) 8-foot long planks stacked on each other for the other long side of our rectangular frame

- Three (3) 8-foot long planks each cut in half to make a total of six (6) 4-foot long planks

  1. (3) 4-foot long planks stacked on each other for one short side of our rectangular frame
  2. (3) 4-foot planks stacked on each other for the other short side of our rectangular frame

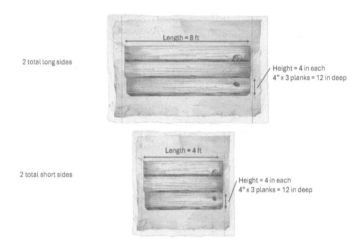

Figure 2 Wooden raised bed example dimensions

- If reinforcing the corners (recommended) cut the additional 4"x4" wood plank to 12 inches in length each for a total of four (4) pieces, one for each corner of the rectangular frame.

2. Assemble the frame:

- Lay out the planks on a flat surface.
- Butt the long ends against the short ends to create a rectangle frame, like the frame of a sandbox.

- Drill at least two pilot holes at each end of the long planks, two on the left side and two on the right side (for a total of 4 holes/plank).

  - The holes as measured from the top of the plank should be approximately 1 inch and 3 inches down from the top.
  - Then use these pilot holes to drill screws through the long plank into its abutting short plank securely.

- Stack the 3 rectangular frames one on top of the other. Screw the wooden reinforcement pieces vertically inside each corner as shown in the picture below.

Figure 3 Raised bed with reinforced corners
awaiting third rectangular frame

3. Prepare the site: If not performed previously, clear the area where the bed will be placed, removing any weeds or large stones. Level the ground as much as possible.

4. Position the frame and secure: Place the frame in the prepared site. Check with a level and adjust as necessary by adding or removing soil underneath. Once in place, you can add a few stakes driven into the ground inside the bed for further stability.

5. Line it: Line the bottom of the bed with landscape fabric to prevent weeds from growing up into the bed and to keep the soil contained. Secure this with a staple gun. For a more economical solution, line the bottom of the bed with cardboard or newspaper.

DIY Raised Bed from Recycled Material

Consider building a raised bed from untreated wooden pallets for an eco-friendly and cost-effective option. Here's how:

1. **Collect pallets:** Ensure they are untreated and free from any chemical residue.
2. **Dismantle the pallets:** Carefully take apart the pallets to retrieve the usable wood slats.
3. **Cut to size and assemble:** Follow the steps outlined above for building with new wood, using the reclaimed wood slats. You might need to sand down the wood to prevent splinters.

Building a raised bed, whether from new or recycled materials, is a project that can greatly enhance your gardening experience. It's a straightforward way to create a tailored space for your plants to thrive, providing them with a nutrient-rich environment while saving you from the strain of traditional in-ground gardening. With your new raised bed ready, you're set to begin planting and reaping the rewards of your efforts.

1.6 Where Do I Put My Raised Bed?

Deciding where to place your raised bed is much more than just picking a spot in your garden or yard—it's about understanding the unique needs of the plants you wish to grow and making the most of the space you have. Sunlight, for instance, is the lifeblood of your garden. Most vegetables and flowers thrive in full sunlight, requiring at least six (6) to eight (8) hours of direct sun per day. However, certain plants might need partial shade, especially in hotter climates where the intense midday sun can be more harmful than beneficial. Observing how sunlight plays across your potential garden spot over the course of a day will give you invaluable insights into where your raised bed should go.

Start by spending a day noting the areas that receive the most consistent sunlight. This can be as simple as checking different spots in your yard or balcony at various times— morning, noon, and late afternoon—to see how the shadows change. The sun's path will shift slightly with the seasons, so an area that's sunny now might be shaded during other parts of the year. If you're planning for year-round gardening, consider this seasonal shift. A south-facing location usually receives the most light year-round and is ideal for most garden plants.

Space efficiency is another critical factor. Raised beds can be built in various sizes, but they should be proportionate to the space available. In smaller gardens or on balconies, a single small raised bed or several narrow ones might be more practical than one large bed. The key is to maximize your growing area without overcrowding the space, ensuring each plant has enough room to grow without competition for sunlight, nutrients, or water. Arranging your beds in a layout that allows you easy access for planting, watering, and harvesting is just as important. Ideally, you should be able to reach the center of the raised bed from all sides, or at least from two sides if the bed is against a wall.

When dealing with less-than-ideal lighting or space conditions, creativity and flexibility are your best tools. If your garden area suffers from inadequate lighting, consider plants that can thrive in partial shade, such as leafy greens (e.g., spinach and kale) or root vegetables (e.g., carrots and potatoes). For spaces that get a mix of sun and shade, arrange your plants so that those requiring the most light are placed in the sunniest part of the bed, with shade-tolerant plants in less exposed areas.

Sometimes, the ideal spot for a raised bed might be on a slope or uneven ground. In such cases, leveling the ground where you will place your raised bed is important to prevent water from pooling on one side and ensure even soil moisture throughout the bed. If leveling the ground is not an option, designing your raised bed with a tiered structure can be a practical and visually appealing solution. This manages sloping ground effectively and also adds an interesting architectural element to your garden.

In urban settings, where space is at a premium, making efficient use of every inch is essential. Vertical gardening techniques, trellises, and climbing plants can expand your growing space upwards, freeing up valuable ground area for your raised beds. We will explore these options below and vertical gardening specifically in **Section 1.8 What Is Vertical Gardening**.

By observing your area's specific conditions and thoughtfully planning your raised bed placement, you can overcome most gardening challenges. Whether you're working with a sprawling backyard or a modest balcony, the right location for your raised bed can lead to a thriving garden that enhances your home and brings satisfaction through every season. Each choice you make in planning your garden setup not only affects plant health and yield but also how you interact with and enjoy your garden daily.

1.7 Where Do I Put My Containers?

When it comes to arranging your container garden, the key is to think about practicality just as much as aesthetics. Where you place your containers can greatly influence how well your plants will grow, and how easily you can care for them. Let's explore some crucial considerations like water drainage, physical accessibility, and how to make the most out of the space you have.

Water Drainage Considerations

Proper drainage is critical in container gardening. Unlike in-ground beds where excess water can disperse throughout the surrounding soil, containers can trap water, leading to water-logged soil that can suffocate plant roots. To prevent this, ensure every container has adequate drainage holes. But where does the water go once it drains out? This is where placement comes into play. Position containers in areas where water can easily drain away without causing damage or inconvenience. For instance, avoid placing containers directly on untreated wooden decks where prolonged moisture can cause rot. Instead, consider placing them on cement patios, gravel paths, or on raised platforms with trays underneath to catch the runoff. This setup keeps your plants healthy and your spaces clean, preventing water from pooling where it shouldn't.

Figure 4 Container with stand and drip tray and containers with a drip tray

For balconies or indoor settings, water drainage necessitates careful planning to avoid dripping onto neighbors or indoor floors. Drip trays or self-watering containers are solutions that can help manage water effectively, keeping both your plants and home environment tidy and dry. Always check the capacity of the drip trays to ensure they can handle the water output without overflowing during heavy watering or rain.

Physical Limitations

Gardening should be a source of joy, not strain. For those with physical limitations, the ease of access to containers is a significant consideration. Place containers at heights that reduce the need to bend or stretch excessively. Using stands or platforms to elevate containers to waist or chest height makes gardening more comfortable and accessible for everyone, especially if you have back issues or use a wheelchair.

Moreover, the layout of containers should allow for easy movement between them. Ensure there's enough space to walk, maneuver a wheelchair, or use garden tools without obstacles. For individuals with visual impairments, containers with tactile or brightly colored edges can help in identifying garden boundaries and plant locations, enhancing the gardening experience through improved navigation and interaction.

Maximizing Space

In many urban homes, space is at a premium, but a lack of space doesn't mean you can't have a thriving garden. The strategic placement and choice of containers can maximize both plant health and garden productivity.

- Use tiered plant stands or ladder shelves to create vertical growing areas that can accommodate more plants without sprawling horizontally. This saves floor space and adds visual interest to your garden, drawing the eye upward and making the area feel larger.
- Hanging baskets are another fantastic option for small spaces. They can be hung from balconies, window ledges, or ceiling hooks to beautify otherwise unused space.
- Similarly, rail planters are perfect for balcony gardens, as they can be securely attached to railings, maximizing your usable planting area without taking up floor space.

Figure 5 *Tiered plant stand, hanging baskets, and rail planter*

In areas where floor space is available, consider grouping containers closely to create microclimates where plants can benefit from shared shade and humidity, further enhancing growth and vitality.

Vertical planting is a great solution if you're working with limited space or want to add a creative element to your garden. Vining plants like peas, beans, and cucumbers thrive in vertical systems, using trellises or supports to climb. This saves space, promotes better air circulation around the plants, and reduces the risk of disease. However, not all plants are suited for vertical growing. Root vegetables, for instance, need deep, stable soil to develop properly, so they are best grown in traditional beds or deep containers.

When arranging containers, consider the needs of the plants. Taller plants should be placed where they won't cast shade on shorter, sun-loving plants. Rotating pots regularly ensures that all sides of your plants receive equal light, promoting even growth and preventing the "leaning" effect as plants stretch toward the light source.

Don't be afraid to move your containers around, especially if you see plants struggling in the areas you've initially placed them in. The whole point with containers is the flexibility of movement, so use placement to your advantage and see where your plants are happiest.

In essence, the thoughtful placement of containers can transform even the smallest spaces into bountiful gardens. By considering factors such as water drainage, physical accessibility, and space efficiency, you can create a container garden that is not only productive but also a delightful, stress-free sanctuary. Whether you are tending to fragrant herbs, vibrant flowers, or hearty vegetables, the right setup allows you to cultivate a thriving garden tailored to fit your lifestyle and physical needs.

1.8 What is Vertical Gardening?

Vertical gardening, a brilliant solution for small and unconventional spaces, transforms walls and fences into lush, productive greenery. This method involves growing plants upwards using trellises, wall-mounted containers, towers, or stacked systems, rather than spreading them out over the ground. This style of gardening is a space-saver and a dynamic way to add visual interest to your home or garden, creating living art that breathes life into every corner.

Vertical gardens can be both indoor and outdoor, with each setting offering unique benefits and considerations.

- Indoors, vertical gardens can purify the air and add a touch of nature to your living space, which is especially valuable in urban environments where outdoor space may be limited or non-existent. They can be integrated into the design of your home as decorative elements or as functional parts of your living space, where herbs and greens can be grown within easy reach of your kitchen. However, indoor vertical gardening does require attention to lighting, as many indoor environments do not provide sufficient light for photosynthesis. This might necessitate the use of grow lights, which can increase the complexity and cost of your garden.
- Outdoors, vertical gardens can transform bare walls, fences, or balconies into productive spaces. They can provide privacy, reduce heat from direct sunlight, and even help insulate your home. Outdoor vertical

gardens do need to be planned with exposure to the elements in mind, ensuring they have protection during harsh weather and adequate sunlight for the plants being grown.

When it comes to setting up a vertical garden, you have the option to either purchase ready-made vertical gardening units or build one yourself. Ready-made units are available at most garden centers and online gardening or retail stores. These can range in price from around $50 for simple systems to upwards of $200 or more for larger, more intricate setups. These pre-built solutions are great for those who prefer a quick and easy setup, as they often come with all necessary components and instructions.

Figure 6 Examples of Indoor and Outdoor Vertical Gardening

Building your own vertical gardening unit offers personal customization and can often be more cost-effective. You can use materials such as recycled wooden pallets, PVC pipes, or metal grids. For a basic DIY vertical garden using a wooden pallet, you will need:

- One wooden pallet (ensure it is heat-treated rather than chemically treated for safety)

- Landscape fabric
- Staple gun and staples
- Optional: paint or wood stain for aesthetics

To construct, staple the landscape fabric to the back, bottom, and sides of the pallet to form a container that will hold the soil. If you wish, paint or stain the wood first for a more polished look. This type of vertical garden is perfect for herbs, succulents, or small flowers and can be leaned against a wall or hung.

Figure 7 DIY Vertical Garden Space Using a
Recycled Wood Pallet

If you have children or pets, it's important to consider safety and accessibility when installing a vertical garden. Ensure that any wall-mounted systems are securely fastened to avoid accidents. Avoid using toxic plants or those with sharp edges in areas where children or pets play. Additionally, place delicate plants higher up where they can't be easily reached by curious hands or paws. Always check that the materials used in your vertical garden, such as paints or stains, are non-toxic and safe for indoor use.

Vertical gardening is a versatile and engaging way to garden that fits into the modern lifestyle, especially for those with limited space. Whether you craft a hanging herb garden in your kitchen or a floral display on your balcony, the vertical element introduces a new dimension to gardening that encourages creativity and experimentation. As you watch your vertical garden thrive, you'll not only enjoy the practical benefits of fresh produce and beautiful blooms but also the improved aesthetics and environmental quality of your living space.

1.9 What Kind of Plants Do I Put in My Garden?

Deciding what to plant in your garden is synonymous to setting the table for a feast—it's all about what you enjoy, what nourishes you, and what thrives in your care. Before you even put a seed in the soil, consider what you want from your garden. Are you looking to add vibrant splashes of color with flowers, provide fresh herbs for your culinary adventures, or harvest your own vegetables? Maybe you're dreaming of a garden that does a little bit of everything. Your goals will guide your choices, helping you create a garden that is beautiful, productive, and deeply satisfying to tend.

For those of you just starting out, simplicity and success are key. You'll want to choose plants known for their resilience and ease of care. Vegetables such as radishes, lettuce, and spinach are nearly foolproof and provide quick gratification, maturing in as little as 30 days. Tomatoes and bell peppers take longer to bear fruit, but their needs are straightforward. For fruits, consider strawberries and blueberries, which can be grown in containers if you're short on space. When it comes to flowers, sunflowers, marigolds, and pansies are easy to care for and bring a delightful splash of color to your garden. All of these are easy to care for in both raised beds and containers.

Companion planting is a fantastic way to enhance your garden's health and yield. This practice involves placing plants together that benefit each other in various ways. Certain plants can help deter unwanted insects or attract beneficial ones. Incorporating these plants into your garden helps maintain a natural balance, reducing your need for chemical pesticides. For example, marigolds emit a natural substance from their roots that deters nematodes, tiny soil-dwelling pests that can harm tomato plants. Planting basil near your tomatoes improves their flavor as well as helps repel flies and mosquitoes. Lavender and chrysanthemums contain natural compounds that repel bugs, while plants like dill and fennel attract ladybugs, which eat aphids. Additionally, consider plants such as marigolds and nasturtiums, which are not only beautiful but also work as "trap crops", attracting pests away from more valuable plants. Natural pest control is an integral part of maintaining a healthy garden.

It is also wise to be aware of incompatible pairings. Keep onions and beans separate, as they can inhibit each other's growth. Similarly, carrots should be kept away from dill, as the two can stunt each other's development.

Below is a table listing some common plants that benefit from being planted close together and another table listing those that should not be placed near one another. In the first table, if the "Good with" is blank, that means that there are numerous plants that can benefit from the items listed in the "Benefits" column. Companion planting is a large topic and we will only touch on it briefly with these two tables.

Beneficial Companions

Table 1: Example Beneficial Companion Plants		
Plant	Good with	Benefits
Allamanda		Attracts pollinators: butterflies and hummingbirds
Basil	Tomatoes and Peppers	Improves flavor; repels insects such as whiteflies, mosquitoes, spider mites, and aphids
Bee Balm		Attracts pollinators: bees, butterflies, and hummingbirds
Bell Peppers	Onions and Parsley	Deters pests
Black-eyed Susan		Attracts pollinators: butterflies and bees
Blueberries	Hydrangeas	Helps monitor soil acidity
Borage	Strawberries	Improves growth and flavor; attracts beneficial insects
Calendula		Repels whiteflies and attracts beneficial insects
Cantaloupe	Marigolds	Deters pests
Chamomile		Attracts beneficial insects
Chives	Roses	Enhances rose bush growth Deters Japanese beetles
Chrysanthemum		Repels beetles
Cilantro	Spinach and Beans	Deters aphids
Coreopsis		Attracts pollinators: bees and butterflies
Coneflower		Attracts pollinators
Dill	Cabbage, Onions, and Cucumbers	Attracts beneficial insects
Fennel		Attracts beneficial insects
Foxglove		Attracts pollinators: hummingbirds
Ixora		Attracts pollinators: butterflies
Lavender		Attracts pollinators, repels insects
Lettuce	Strawberries	Attracts pests that might otherwise target strawberries; can be planted close together for space efficiency

Marigold	Tomatoes, Peppers	Attracts beneficial insects such as hoverflies, bees, and butterflies, controls aphids, and deters nematodes
Mint	Cabbage and Tomatoes	Repels cabbage moths and aphids
Nasturtiums	Beans, Cucumbers, Tomatoes, and other edible plants	Attracts aphids away from beans and blackflies away from edible plants; flowers are edible
Parsley	Tomatoes and Asparagus	Enhances growth and flavor; attracts beneficial insects
Petunias	Vegetables and other flowers	Attracts pollinators and beneficial insects
Rosemary	Beans, Cabbage, and Carrots	Repels a variety of pests
Sage	Carrots and Cabbage	Repels carrot flies and reduces injury from cabbage moths
Sunflower	Cucumbers, Squash, and Corn	Attracts pollinators; provides support for climbing plants; provides shade for sun-stressed plants
Sweet Pea	Vegetables and other flowers	Attracts pollinators and deters pests
Thyme	Strawberries	Deters worms that affect the fruit
Watermelon	Radishes	Deters pests

Groupings to Avoid

Table 2: Example Groupings to Avoid		
Plant	Avoid with	Why
Bell Peppers	Beans, cauliflower, broccoli, cabbage, bok choy, kohlrabi, brussel sprouts, kale	Stunt each other's growth
Carrots	Dill	Stunt each other's development
Onions	Beans	Inhibit each other's growth
Peppers	Beans	Potential competition and entanglement issues

Choosing the right plants for your garden is about more than just aesthetics or yield. It's about creating a space that reflects your tastes, meets your needs, and brings you pleasure every day. Whether you're filling your kitchen with fresh herbs, cutting flowers to brighten your home, or harvesting vegetables for family meals, the right choices can turn gardening into a rewarding and enriching experience.

As you select your plants, consider their needs and compatibilities, and plan your garden layout to support healthy growth and abundant harvests. With a little planning and care, your garden will flourish, providing you with a beautiful and productive oasis. The next section will help you determine which vegetables, flowers, and fruit grow best at which temperatures and during which seasons based upon your climate zone.

1.10 What are Climate (Hardiness) Zones and Why are They Important?

Understanding climate zones is having the roadmap for your gardening adventure—it guides you in choosing the right plants that will thrive in your specific environment. Essentially, climate zones are defined areas that share similar average temperatures, rainfall, and other climatic factors. These zones are crucial for garden planning because they help predict which plants will flourish and which might struggle. This section may seem overwhelming, but keep in mind that I included all of the world's zones simply for completeness. You only need to find your zone and focus your attention on growing in that particular zone.

The USDA Hardiness Zone map divides North America into 13 primary zones, each representing a 10-degree Fahrenheit difference in **average annual minimum winter temperature.** Find your zone below.

Table 3: USDA Hardiness Zone Numbers, Temperature Ranges, and Associated States

Zone	Temperature Range	States
1	-60°F to -50°F	North parts of Alaska
2	-50°F to -40°F	Central parts of Alaska
3	-40°F to -30°F	Northern parts of Minnesota, North Dakota, Montana, and southern parts of Alaska
4	-30°F to -20°F	Wisconsin, Northern Iowa, parts of New York, New Hampshire, and Maine
5	-20°F to -10°F	Illinois, Ohio, Missouri, Pennsylvania, Connecticut, and parts of Colorado
6	-10°F to 0°F	Kentucky, Maryland, parts of Virginia and Massachusetts
7	0°F to 10°F	Tennessee, North Carolina, Arkansas, parts of Texas and New Jersey
8	10°F to 20°F	Northern Florida, Georgia, South Carolina, parts of Oregon and Texas
9	20°F to 30°F	Southern Florida, Louisiana, southern parts of Texas, parts of California
10	30°F to 40°F	Southern Florida, southernmost parts of Texas and California
11	40°F to 50°F	Hawaii, parts of Southern Florida
12	50°F to 60°F	Hawaii, Puerto Rico
13	60°F to 70°F	Hawaii (tropical regions)

The following tables can be used as guides for choosing vegetables, flowers, and fruit to grow in your garden based on your particular growing zone and season in the US. **Table 4** provides examples of vegetables, flowers, and fruit that can be grown in your particular US Zone. **Table 5** provides examples of the types of vegetables that can be grown in your particular US Zone based on the seasons of Spring, Summer, Fall, and Winter. **Table 6** provides examples of the types of flowers that can be grown in your particular US Zone based on the seasons. **Table 7** provides examples of the types of fruit that can be grown in your particular US Zone based on the seasons. In this way, wherever you may live and whenever you start your gardening journey, you'll be setting yourself up for success!

Table 4: Example Vegetables, Flowers, and Fruit by USDA Hardiness Zone

Zone	Example Vegetables	Example Flowers	Example Fruit
1	Kale, Carrots, Spinach	Arctic Poppy, Moss Campion	None
2	Lettuce, Turnips, Radishes	Pasque Flower, Saxifrage	Cloudberry, Arctic Raspberry
3	Cabbage, Beets, Peas	Lupine, Snow-in-Summer, Blanket Flower	Apples, Cherries, Raspberries
4	Broccoli, Brussels Sprouts, Onions	Daylily, Iris, Yarrow	Pears, Plums, Strawberries
5	Tomatoes, Peppers, Squash	Peony, Coneflower, Bee Balm	Grapes, Blueberries, Blackberries
6	Cucumbers, Eggplant, Beans	Hosta, Coreopsis, Black-Eyed Susan	Peaches, Apples, Kiwi
7	Sweet Potatoes, Okra, Melons	Hydrangea, Azalea, Clematis	Figs, Pomegranates, Persimmons
8	Corn, Peppers, Tomatoes	Camellias, Gardenia, Lavender	Citrus (Lemons, Oranges), Figs, Pomegranates
9	Eggplant, Beans, Sweet Corn	Bougainvillea, Hibiscus, Bird of Paradise	Avocados, Grapefruit, Pineapple Guava
10	Tomatoes, Bell Peppers, Zucchini	Orchids, Plumeria, Heliconia	Bananas, Mangoes, Papayas
11	Malabar Spinach, Hot Peppers, Yardlong Beans	Anthurium, Bromeliads, Tropical Lilies	Guava, Passionfruit, Lychee
12	Tropical Spinach, Taro, Okra	Hibiscus, Ixora, Allamanda	Soursop
13	Cassava, Sweet Potatoes, Tropical Squash	Plumeria, Bougainvillea, Ginger	Coconut, Rambutan

Table 5: Example Vegetables by USDA Hardiness Zone and Season

Zone	Example Spring Vegetables	Example Summer Vegetables	Example Fall Vegetables	Example Winter Vegetables
1	Kale, Spinach, Carrots	None	Kale, Spinach, Carrots	None
2	Lettuce, Radishes, Spinach	None	Lettuce, Radishes, Spinach	None
3	Peas, Broccoli, Beets	Tomatoes, Peppers, Zucchini	Cabbage, Carrots, Spinach	None
4	Lettuce, Radishes, Broccoli	Tomatoes, Peppers, Cucumbers	Kale, Brussels Sprouts, Turnips	Spinach, Carrots, Cabbage
5	Lettuce, Radishes, Peas	Tomatoes, Peppers, Beans	Broccoli, Cabbage, Kale	Spinach, Carrots, Onions
6	Lettuce, Spinach, Radishes	Tomatoes, Peppers, Cucumbers	Broccoli, Cauliflower, Brussels Sprouts	Spinach, Carrots, Kale
7	Lettuce, Spinach, Peas	Tomatoes, Eggplant, Beans	Broccoli, Cauliflower, Kale	Spinach, Carrots, Brussels Sprouts
8	Lettuce, Spinach, Broccoli	Tomatoes, Peppers, Okra	Broccoli, Cauliflower, Lettuce	Spinach, Carrots, Kale
9	Lettuce, Spinach, Peas	Tomatoes, Peppers, Eggplant	Broccoli, Cauliflower, Lettuce	Spinach, Carrots, Kale
10	Lettuce, Spinach, Peas	Tomatoes, Peppers, Eggplant	Broccoli, Cauliflower, Lettuce	Spinach, Carrots, Kale
11	Lettuce, Spinach, Peas	Tomatoes, Peppers, Eggplant	Broccoli, Cauliflower, Lettuce	Spinach, Carrots, Kale
12	Lettuce, Spinach, Peas	Tomatoes, Peppers, Eggplant	Broccoli, Cauliflower, Lettuce	Spinach, Carrots, Kale
13	Lettuce, Spinach, Peas	Tomatoes, Peppers, Eggplant	Broccoli, Cauliflower, Lettuce	Spinach, Carrots, Kale

Table 6: Example Flowers by USDA Hardiness Zone and Season				
Zone	Example Spring Flowers	Example Summer Flowers	Example Fall Flowers	Example Winter Flowers
1	Arctic Poppy, Moss Campion	None	Arctic Poppy, Moss Campion	None
2	Pasque Flower, Saxifrage	None	Pasque Flower, Saxifrage	None
3	Lupine, Snow-in-Summer, Blanket Flower	Zinnia, Marigold, Petunia	Aster, Chrysanthemum, Sedum	None
4	Tulips, Daffodils, Hyacinths	Coneflower, Black-Eyed Susan, Daylily	Aster, Chrysanthemum, Sedum	None
5	Peony, Iris, Lily-of-the-Valley	Sunflower, Zinnia, Marigold	Aster, Chrysanthemum, Sedum	Hellebore, Snowdrops, Winter Jasmine
6	Daffodils, Crocus, Tulips	Dahlia, Gloriosa Daisy, Lavender	Aster, Chrysanthemum, Sedum	Hellebore, Snowdrops, Winter Jasmine
7	Daffodils, Crocus, Tulips	Dahlia, Gloriosa Daisy, Lavender	Aster, Chrysanthemum, Sedum	Hellebore, Snowdrops, Winter Jasmine
8	Daffodils, Crocus, Tulips	Hibiscus, Gardenia, Lavender	Aster, Chrysanthemum, Sedum	Hellebore, Snowdrops, Winter Jasmine
9	Daffodils, Crocus, Tulips	Hibiscus, Gardenia, Lavender	Aster, Chrysanthemum, Sedum	Hellebore, Snowdrops, Winter Jasmine
10	Daffodils, Crocus, Tulips	Bougainvillea, Hibiscus, Marigold	Aster, Chrysanthemum, Sedum	Hellebore, Snowdrops, Winter Jasmine
11	Daffodils, Crocus, Tulips	Bougainvillea, Hibiscus, Marigold	Aster, Chrysanthemum, Sedum	Hellebore, Snowdrops, Winter Jasmine
12	Daffodils, Crocus, Tulips	Bougainvillea, Hibiscus, Marigold	Aster, Chrysanthemum, Sedum	Hellebore, Snowdrops, Winter Jasmine
13	Daffodils, Crocus, Tulips	Bougainvillea, Hibiscus, Marigold	Aster, Chrysanthemum, Sedum	Hellebore, Snowdrops, Winter Jasmine

Zone	Example Spring Fruit	Example Summer Fruit	Example Fall Fruit	Example Winter Fruit
\multicolumn{5}{l}{**Table 7: Example Fruit by USDA Hardiness Zone and Season**}
1	None	None	None	None
2	None	None	None	None
3	Rhubarb	Strawberries, Raspberries	Apples, Pears	None
4	Rhubarb	Strawberries, Raspberries, Blueberries	Apples, Pears	None
5	Rhubarb, Cherries	Strawberries, Raspberries, Blueberries	Apples, Pears, Grapes	None
6	Rhubarb, Cherries	Strawberries, Blueberries, Peaches	Apples, Pears, Grapes	None
7	Strawberries, Cherries	Blueberries, Peaches, Blackberries	Apples, Pears, Grapes	None
8	Strawberries, Cherries	Blueberries, Peaches, Blackberries	Apples, Pears, Grapes	Citrus (Lemons, Oranges, Grapefruit)
9	Strawberries, Cherries	Blueberries, Peaches, Blackberries	Apples, Pears, Grapes	Citrus (Lemons, Oranges, Grapefruit)
10	Strawberries, Cherries	Blueberries, Peaches, Blackberries	Apples, Pears, Grapes, Figs	Citrus (Lemons, Oranges, Grapefruit)
11	Strawberries	Bananas, Mangoes, Papayas	Figs, Pomegranates	Citrus (Lemons, Oranges, Grapefruit)
12	Strawberries	Bananas, Mangoes, Papayas	Figs, Pomegranates	Citrus (Lemons, Oranges, Grapefruit)
13	Strawberries	Bananas, Mangoes, Papayas	Figs, Pomegranates	Citrus (Lemons, Oranges, Grapefruit)

Canada uses a zone/subzone system that ranges from 0a (extremely cold) to 10 (mild climate). These zones are based on minimum winter temperatures, maximum summer temperatures, rainfall, snow cover, and wind speed. Listed in the table below alongside the Canadian zones are the comparable USDA Hardiness Zones numbers. *A word of warning, these are simply estimates as Canadian zones are calculated differently from US zones as described above.

Table 8: Canadian Hardiness Zone Numbers with Comparable* USDA Hardiness Zone Numbers, Temperature Ranges, and Associated Provinces

Zone	USDA	Temperature Range	Provinces
0a	1	below -51.1°C (-60°F)	Northern regions of Nunavut
1a,b	2	-51.1°C to -45.5°C (-60°F to -50°F)	Northern regions of Yukon, Northwest Territories, and parts of Nunavut
2a,b	3	-45.5°C to -40°C (-50°F to -40°F)	Central and southern Yukon, southern parts of Northwest Territories, northern Alberta, northern Saskatchewan, and northern Manitoba
3a,b	4 (3a) 5 (3b)	-40°C to -34.5°C (-40°F to -30°F)	Southern Alberta, southern Saskatchewan, southern Manitoba, and northern parts of Ontario and Quebec
4a,b	5 (4b)	-34.5°C to -28.9°C (-30°F to -20°F)	Central Alberta, southern Ontario, and southern Quebec
5a,b	6	-28.9°C to -23.3°C (-20°F to -10°F)	Central and southern Ontario, southern Quebec, and parts of New Brunswick, Nova Scotia, and Prince Edward Island
6a,b	7	-23.3°C to -17.8°C (-10°F to -0°F)	Southern Ontario, southern Quebec, southern New Brunswick, Nova Scotia, and parts of Newfoundland
7a,b	8	-17.8°C to -12.3°C (0°F to 10°F)	Coastal British Columbia, including Vancouver Island and the Lower Mainland
8a,b	9	-12.3°C to -6.6°C (10°F to 20°F)	Coastal areas of British Columbia, including Vancouver and Victoria
9a	10	-6.6°C to -3.9°C (20°F to 25°F)	Limited areas along the southern coastal regions of British Columbia
9b	10	-3.9°C to -1.1°C (25°F to 30°F)	Southern coastal areas of British Columbia, particularly parts of Vancouver Island and the Gulf Islands
10	11	-1.1°C to 3.9°C (30°F to 39°F)	Southern coastal areas of British Columbia, southern Vancouver Island and southern Gulf Islands

Internationally, the Köppen climate classification system includes broader zones (climates) such as tropical, arid, temperate, continental, polar, and highland. Each climate has sub-categories based on specific climate conditions.

Table 9: International Climate Classification System and Associated Countries

Climate	Subclimate	Conditions	Countries
Tropical	Tropical Rainforest (Af)	High temperatures and heavy rainfall year-round	Brazil, Indonesia, Malaysia, Democratic Republic of Congo
	Tropical Monsoon (Am)	High temperatures, significant seasonal rainfall differences with a short dry season	India, Thailand, parts of West Africa
	Tropical Savanna (Aw/As)	High temperatures, distinct wet and dry seasons	Brazil (Cerrado), India (central and southern parts), Kenya, Tanzania
Arid	Hot Desert (BWh)	Extremely low precipitation, very high temperatures	Egypt, Saudi Arabia, Australia (central regions)
	Cold Desert (BWk)	Low precipitation, significant temperature differences between summer and winter	Mongolia (Gobi Desert), parts of Iran, Kazakhstan
	Hot Steppe (Bsh)	Low precipitation, hot summers	Sahel region in Africa, parts of Australia, southwestern United States
	Cold Steppe (BSk)	Low precipitation, cold winters	Central Asia, parts of Canada, parts of Russia
Temperate	Humid Subtropical (Cfa)	Hot, humid summers and mild winters	Southeastern United States, China (south and east), Japan
	Oceanic/Marine West Coast (Cfb)	Mild temperatures, rainfall throughout the year	United Kingdom, New Zealand, Western Europe
	Subpolar Oceanic (Cfc)	Cool temperatures, rainfall throughout the year	Coastal areas of Iceland, parts of Scotland, southern Chile
	Mediterranean/Hot Summer (Csa)	Hot, dry summers and mild, wet winters	Italy, Greece, California (in the US), parts of Spain
	Mediterranean/Warm Summer (Csb)	Warm, dry summers and mild, wet winters	Portugal, parts of California (in the US), central Chile

Continental	Humid Continental/ Hot Summer (Dfa)	Hot summers, cold winters, significant precipitation year-round	Eastern United States, parts of China, South Korea
	Humid Continental/ Warm Summer (Dfb)	Warm summers, cold winters, significant precipitation year-round	Canada (southern parts), Russia (western parts), Northern Japan
	Subarctic (Dfc)	Very cold winters, mild summers, low precipitation	Canada (northern parts), Russia (Siberia), parts of Scandinavia
	Subarctic with Dry Winter (Dfd/Dwd)	Extremely cold winters, mild summers, low precipitation, especially in winter	Central Siberia
Polar	Tundra (ET)	Very cold temperatures year-round, short summers	Greenland (coastal areas), northern Canada, parts of Alaska (in the US)
	Ice Cap (EF)	Perennial ice and snow, extremely cold temperatures	Antarctica, Greenland (interior)
Highland		Climate varies with altitude, generally cooler and wetter than surrounding lowlands	Nepal (Himalayas), Ethiopia (Highlands), Peru (Andes), Switzerland (Alps)

1.11 What Are Microclimates?

Identifying your specific microclimate takes this a step further. Microclimates are small areas within climate zones that have slightly different conditions due to factors such as elevation, proximity to water bodies, or urban development. For example, your garden might be in a particularly windy corridor or in a sunny spot against a south-facing wall that retains heat. Such variations can significantly influence what you can grow successfully.

To identify your garden's microclimate, observe the area through different times of the day and during various weather conditions. Notice if certain parts are prone to frost or if some areas get waterlogged during rain. Such observations can help tailor your gardening strategies, like planting frost-sensitive plants in protected areas or improving drainage where water pools.

Seasonal adjustments are pivotal in gardening. As your climate zone transitions through seasons, your gardening practices should also adapt. In spring, the focus might be on planting frost-tolerant annuals or starting seeds indoors in regions with a short growing season. Summer might require implementing watering systems to combat heat, while fall is ideal for planting perennials that will bloom the following year. Winter in colder zones might involve mulching to protect plants from freezing temperatures. Each season holds its tasks, and understanding your climate zone's seasonal patterns ensures you're always one step ahead.

When selecting plants, always consider their compatibility with your climate zone and microclimate. Each plant has specific needs in terms of temperature, sunlight, and water. For instance, succulents are perfect for arid, sunny zones but might struggle in a damp, shadowy area. Conversely, ferns thrive in the shade and might burn in direct sunlight. Local garden centers are invaluable resources, as they typically stock plants suited to the local climate. Additionally, many gardening books and websites offer plant selectors based on climate zones, simplifying your choices. I've included **Chapter 6 Plant Profiles** to assist you in making educated choices and to set expectations. As much as I would love to have my beloved bougainvillea in my garden in the Northeast, this is just not a flower that will grow in my climate zone!

By considering these factors—climate zones, microclimates, seasonal changes, and plant selection—you can create a garden that thrives. Tailoring your garden to fit its climatic context means less struggle with unsuitable plants and more enjoyment and success in your gardening endeavors. Whether you're tending a lush vegetable garden, a fragrant herb patch, or a vibrant flower bed, understanding and working with your climate zone is key to achieving a flourishing garden.

1.12 Wrapping Up Chapter 1

In this chapter, we've covered the basics, such as defining the different types of gardening and creating and choosing the elements for each type. We've talked about garden placement, types of plants, climate zones, as well as DIY garden elements. We've reviewed a lot of information, but don't be overwhelmed! Remember, you don't ever need to memorize this information. This book is your guide and you can reference it as much and as many times as you need to—that's what it's here for! Stay the course and you will be rewarded!

You may also be thinking this all sounds great, but time-consuming. There is undoubtedly upfront work involved in getting a garden started from scratch. Start small and add to your garden as time and effort allow. Once established, a garden can be a time saver. I remember all the times basil was needed for a recipe and I just didn't have it. Going to the grocery store at the last-minute was time-consuming and stressful. Or times when I ran out of lettuce to make a salad... or tomatoes...or cucumbers. What's better than getting these fresh from your garden within steps of your kitchen?

Our next chapter will build on these basics and will review items such as tools, watering, soil, composting, and other maintenance activities to ensure a healthy and abundant harvest.

TWO

Essential Tools and Techniques

As you embark on your gardening adventure, think of your tools as trusted companions—each one plays a critical role in helping you cultivate a thriving garden. Just as a chef values their knives or an artist their brushes, a gardener's tools are fundamental to their success. This chapter is your guide to assembling the essential toolkit that will empower you to work your soil, plant your seeds, and care for your growing garden with ease.

2.1 What Kind of Tools Do I Absolutely Need?

Basic Toolset

Every gardener, especially when you're just starting out, needs a core set of tools that will cover most gardening tasks. Here's a list of the basics:

- **Gloves:** Protect your hands from thorns, blisters, and dirt. Look for durable yet comfortable gloves that fit well. Consider gloves that are coated (latex, nitrile, rubber) for water resistance, as you will be working with water in some capacity. Working with water-saturated gloves for extended periods of time can be uncomfortable.
- **Spade and Trowel:** These are essential for digging. A spade is perfect for larger jobs such as turning soil, while a trowel is ideal for smaller tasks such as planting and weeding.

  ○ For container gardening, a spade may not be required, as larger jobs may not be applicable.

- **Pruning Shears:** Essential for trimming and shaping plants, and for cutting away dead or overgrown branches.
- **Garden Fork:** This tool is great for breaking up compact soil and for turning compost. This may not be necessary for smaller spaces if your spade and/or trowel will do the trick (such as with container gardening).
- **Watering Can or Hose:** Keeping your plants hydrated is critical, and a watering can with a long spout offers precision, while a hose might be necessary for larger gardens.
- **Rake:** A rake is useful for clearing leaves and debris and for smoothing soil after planting. This also may not be needed if you have a small space or use containers—you can easily pick up leaves and debris

and smooth the soil with swipes of your gloved
hands.

These tools form the backbone of your gardening toolkit,
helping you perform the majority of your gardening tasks
effectively.

Ergonomic Tools

The joy of gardening shouldn't be marred by physical discom-
fort. Ergonomic tools are designed to reduce strain on your
body, making gardening more comfortable and accessible,
especially if you have physical limitations. Ergonomic tools
typically feature padded handles and are shaped to minimize
the effort required to use them. For instance, an ergonomic
trowel may have a curved handle that fits better in your hand,
reducing the risk of strain. Investing in these tools can significantly enhance your gardening experience, keeping it a pleasure and not a pain.

Tools for Any Budget

Gardening doesn't have to be an expensive hobby. While it's
great to invest in high-quality tools that will last, there are
also plenty of ways to save money. For example, many
gardening tools can be found second-hand at garage sales or
online marketplaces. You can also repurpose household items
— old spoons can be turned into markers for your plants, and
milk jugs can be cut into scoops or used to water plants.

If you're on a tight budget, focus on purchasing quality essential tools, and then gradually add to your collection as needed. A few well-chosen tools are often more valuable than a shed full of gadgets that rarely get used.

I personally only have a handful of tools: water-repellant gloves, a trowel, a fork, a watering can, hand-held gardening shears and a weeder. I'm a fanatic weeder, so I have one that has a short handle with an angled head that allows for a more ergonomic way to attack weeds and ensure I am pulling them from their roots.

Tool Maintenance

Taking good care of your tools can extend their life significantly, saving you money in the long run and ensuring they are ready to use when you need them.

- Always clean your tools after use; soil left on metal parts can lead to rust.
- Sharpen blades regularly to keep them effective, especially tools like pruners and shears...remember, work better, not harder!
- Wooden handles can be treated with linseed oil to prevent drying and cracking.
- Store your tools in a dry, protected place to avoid exposure to harsh weather conditions.

Use a mixture of coarse construction sand and oil (mineral, linseed, or WD-40), enough to wet the mixture. Submerge the metal ends of your garden tools after they've been cleaned into the mixture. You can store your tools this way over the winter without them rusting.

Outfitting the Gardener

As a gardener, your personal comfort and safety are just as important as the tools you use. Always wear a hat and apply sunscreen to protect yourself from the sun. Sturdy shoes will protect your feet, and consider waterproof clogs or wellies to keep your feet and socks clean and dry. Knee pads or a kneeling pad can make working at ground level much more comfortable and your knees will thank you the next day. I wear pants with built-in knee pads that work better than moving a kneeling pad around—they have been a game changer! Hydration is critical, so always have a bottle of water close by, especially on hot days.

Equipping yourself with the right tools is the first step toward creating a garden that will bring you fulfillment and nourishment. Just as with any other craft, the quality and suitability of your tools can greatly enhance your efficiency and enjoyment of gardening. With your toolkit ready, you're well-prepared to start digging, planting, and enjoying the fruits of your labor in the beautiful outdoor space you're cultivating.

2.2 Do I Grow From Seed or Do I Use Seedlings?

Deciding between starting your garden from seeds or using seedlings can feel as if you're choosing between baking a cake from scratch or using a pre-made mix. Both options have their merits and can lead to a successful garden, but understanding the nuances can help you make the best choice for your situation. Let's break down the costs, benefits, and some specifics on what grows best from seeds versus seedlings.

Starting with seeds is often more cost-effective. Seeds are generally cheaper than seedlings, especially if you plan to grow a large garden. A single packet of seeds can produce dozens of plants for the same price as one or two pre-grown seedlings. However, growing from seeds requires more time and care, especially in the early stages. Seedlings, on the other hand, offer a head start. They are especially useful if you have a shorter growing season, as they can be planted directly into your garden after the last frost, bypassing the delicate seedling stage where young plants are most vulnerable to weather and pests.

When it comes to what grows well from seeds, many vegetables and flowers are excellent candidates. Radishes, carrots, peas, beans, and leafy greens like lettuce and spinach can go straight into the garden as seeds. These plants often do best when sown directly because they have short germination times and can grow quite quickly. On the flip side, some plants can be challenging to grow from seed due to longer germination times or more complex care needs. For instance, many gardeners prefer to start with seedlings for plants like tomatoes, peppers, and broccoli, which require a longer growing period and might not mature fully if planted late in the season. In **Section 6 Plant Profiles**, the germination times for common vegetables, flowers, and fruit are listed. These times can vary based on temperature, humidity, and seed quality.

Choosing where to buy your seeds or seedlings can also impact your garden's success. Local garden centers often offer varieties that are well-suited to your specific climate and will provide advice on the best planting techniques for your area. Purchasing seeds online can expand your options significantly, allowing you to find rare or specialized varieties that aren't available locally. However, ensure the seeds are from a reputable supplier to avoid poor germination rates or mislabeled species. Seed packets provide a wealth of information crucial for successful planting. They typically include details on when to plant, how deep to plant the seeds, how far apart to space them, and how much light and water they will need. Understanding these instructions is key to helping your plants thrive.

Depending upon where you live and how long it may take the plants you want to plant from seeds to germinate, you may need to invest in grow lights. These are lights that are meant to emulate sunlight and come in an array of designs and prices. If you're looking to germinate just a few containers, these lights can be purchased for somewhere in the $20 range. If you're looking to use them to germinate more plants, shop lights may be a more inexpensive alternative.

Figure 8 A handful of plants under a grow light and many plants under shop lights

If you're wondering what can be planted right now in your garden for immediate success, it largely depends on your local climate and the current season. Refer to the tables in **Section 1.10 What are Climate (Hardiness) Zones and Why are They Important?** to assist in your selection. For most temperate climates, spring is ideal for sowing seeds of frost-tolerant plants like peas and spinach directly into the garden. As the weather warms, you can start seedlings or direct sow seeds of more temperature-sensitive plants like cucumbers and squash. Refer to a local planting calendar to get the most accurate planting times for your specific area.

Navigating the choices between seeds and seedlings doesn't have to be complicated. By considering your gardening goals, the climate you're working with, and how much time you can dedicate to nurturing your plants from seed to sprout, you can make informed decisions that lead to a lush, bountiful garden. Whether you start with a tiny seed or a young plant, the care you provide and the joy of watching your garden grow is what makes gardening such a rewarding endeavor.

2.3 How Do I Grow Seedlings?

If you decide you want to plant seeds, there are a couple of easy and inexpensive ways to accomplish this:

- Use a few paper towels and wet them with water until they are moist but not dripping. Lay the paper towels flat and fold them in half. One half will be used for seeds and the other half will be used to cover the seeds. Place a few seeds on the towel, leaving space in between them. Fold the paper towels over the seeds to cover them, place the paper towels in an empty egg carton, close the lid to create a humid environment, and place in a warm, dark location. Check the paper towels regularly, ensuring they remain moist and adding water as needed.
- A seed starter "kit" can also be used, composed of seed-starting mix and seed trays or small pots. Fill the trays or pots with seed-starting mix, moisten thoroughly, then plant your seeds. Cover the trays or pots with a clear plastic lid or plastic wrap to create a greenhouse effect. Place in a warm, bright location out of direct sunlight.
- Use potting mix or topsoil and place in the spaces of the empty egg carton. Moisten thoroughly, then plant your seeds. Place in a warm, bright location such as a window ledge or use grow lights. Check regularly to ensure the soil remains moist and add water as needed.

2.4 How Do I Water My Plants?

Watering your plants might seem to be the simplest part of gardening, yet it holds profound importance in the health and growth of your garden. Each plant in your lovely garden has its unique thirst level, influenced by its type, the environmental conditions, and its stage of growth. Let's explore how to fine-tune your watering practices to meet these needs effectively, ensuring your garden not only survives but thrives.

Understanding the watering needs of your plants is the first step toward a flourishing garden. Different plants require different amounts of water. For instance, succulents thrive on minimal water, while vegetables such as cucumbers or tomatoes need a steady, more generous supply to produce well. The size of the plant also plays a role; larger plants with deeper roots typically need more water than smaller ones because they have a greater leaf area to support. Additionally, the climate you are gardening in affects how much water your plants need. Hot, dry conditions mean more frequent watering, whereas cooler, cloudy environments might require less. A good rule of thumb is to check the soil. If the top inch of the soil is dry, it's usually a sign that it's time to water. This simple test helps prevent both under and overwatering by ensuring that you're responding directly to your garden's needs.

Seasonal changes demand adjustments in your watering routine. During peak summer months, evaporation rates are high, and plants might need more frequent watering. However, as autumn rolls in and temperatures drop, your plants' water requirements will decrease. This seasonal adjustment is crucial to avoid overwatering, which can be just as detrimental as underwatering. Overwatering can lead to root rot and fungal diseases, while underwatering can stress plants, making them more susceptible to disease and insect attacks. Signs of overwatering include leaves that are soft and discolored; underwatered plants, on the other hand, will have dry, brittle leaves that may turn brown and curl up.

Exploring efficient watering methods can significantly enhance your garden's health and your own conservation efforts. Drip irrigation systems and soaker hoses are excellent for delivering water directly to the soil, reducing waste and minimizing evaporation. These systems can be set up with timers to water your plants at the best time of day, usually early morning or late evening, to further reduce water loss. Another sustainable practice is collecting rainwater. By setting up a rain barrel, you can capture natural rainfall that can be used for watering your garden, which is good for your plants and better for the environment. You can even create a unique ecosystem in your rain barrel by adding fish that will help keep the potential mosquito population down.

Watering container and vertical gardens present unique challenges, primarily due to their confined space and the materials used. Containers and vertical plant setups often dry out faster than in-ground beds and require more frequent monitoring. It's vital to ensure that your containers have good drainage to prevent water from pooling at the roots, which can cause issues like root rot. For vertical gardens, especially those indoors, consider a drip system that can water multiple levels efficiently without over-saturating any one area. This method ensures that all plants receive the right amount of water, from top to bottom, fostering even growth and vitality across your vertical display.

By understanding the specific needs of your plants and adjusting your watering strategies accordingly, you can ensure that every part of your garden receives just the right amount of water to flourish. This mindful approach not only supports the health of your plants but also conserves water—a win for your garden and the planet. As you continue to nurture your garden, remember that watering wisely is key to cultivating a lush, vibrant indoor or outdoor space.

2.5 What Do I Need to Do with the Soil?

First off, what is soil? Most of us think of soil as dirt, the stuff we played in as kids that then turned to mud whenever it rained. Soil is the upper layer of the earth where plants grow and is a mixture of organic material, minerals, gases, liquids, and the organisms that support plant life. In general, there are three types of inorganic material that are components of soil that are broken down roughly by particle size: sand, silt, and clay, with sand being the largest particles and clay being the smallest particles. You will also hear the term "loam" used, which is a balanced mixture of all three and considered ideal for plant growth.

Imagine your garden's soil as a bustling city where every nutrient and microorganism plays a role in maintaining a vibrant ecosystem. Just as a city needs ongoing maintenance and care to thrive, so does your garden's soil. Enhancing the health of your soil isn't just about ensuring your plants have a cozy place to put down roots; it's about creating an environment where they can flourish to their fullest potential.

One of the main advantages of raised bed and container gardening is the ability to control the composition of the materials you put in them, which includes the soil. For raised beds, a mixture of approximately 50% topsoil, 30% compost, and 20% other organic matter works well as a general all-purpose soil. Topsoil is generally loose and loamy. Depending upon the size and number of your raised bed(s), purchasing topsoil in bulk from a garden center may be more cost-effective than purchasing in bags. For containers, a mixture of approximately 35% peat moss, coconut coir, or potting soil; 35% compost; 20% perlite; and 10% vermiculite is recommended.

We talk about compost and how to make your own compost below, but it can be purchased in your local garden center or hardware store. "Other organic matter" includes manure, vermiculture (earthworm castings or yes, earthworm poo!), perlite, vermiculite, coconut coir, and peat moss, which helps break vitamins and minerals down so they're easier to absorb. These materials can be found in abundance at local garden and hardware stores.

Making Your Own Compost

Starting a compost bin is one of the most rewarding projects for any gardener. It's a simple way to recycle your kitchen scraps and yard waste, turning what would otherwise be trash into treasure for your garden. To get started, you'll need a bin or a designated corner of your yard. You can compost a wide variety of organic materials, including fruit and vegetable scraps, coffee grounds, eggshells, grass clippings, and leaves. However, it's important to avoid composting meats, dairy products, and oils, as they can attract pests and create odors. Layer your greens (like kitchen scraps) with your browns (like dry leaves), keeping the pile moist but not overly soggy, and turn it every few weeks to aerate it, which speeds up the decomposition process.

There are many composting options, including containers designed to use a crank or lever to make aerating your compost simple and easy. These can be found at your local garden center or on-line retailer. If you don't have the space for either a ready-made or home-made compost bin, countertop composters can take kitchen and garden scraps and even some compostable "plastics" and turn them into rich compost. I use a countertop composter, and although it was an investment, I'm glad that I added it to my kitchen. No more food waste guilt and lots of amazing compost!

Application Methods for Compost

Introducing compost to your garden is giving your soil a multivitamin. It is packed with nutrients that plants love, and it improves the soil structure, making it easier for roots to grow. The benefits are twofold: it enhances the soil's ability to retain water and nutrients, which is especially helpful during those hot summer months, and it also improves drainage, keeping the root environment balanced so it's never too wet or too dry. Whether you're working with sandy soil that struggles to hold onto water or clay soil that tends to compact and suffocate roots, adding compost can help to balance these extremes, creating ideal growing conditions for almost any plant.

Knowing when and how to apply compost to your garden can make a significant difference in your plants' growth and health. Generally, the best times to add compost are before planting new beds in the early spring and as a top dressing for established plants in the fall. This timing allows the compost to integrate and stabilize within the soil, making nutrients available just as plants are ready to grow. When applying compost, spread a layer about 2-4 inches thick over your garden beds, then gently work it into the top few inches of soil. For containers, spread a thin layer on the surface of the soil around your plants.

Environmental Benefits

Composting offers profound environmental benefits that extend beyond your garden. It reduces the amount of waste that ends up in landfills, which is crucial since organic waste in landfills generates methane, a potent greenhouse gas. By composting, you're enriching your soil and playing a part in reducing global waste and emissions. Moreover, composting encourages a healthier garden ecosystem, reducing the need for chemical fertilizers and pesticides, which can be harmful to both the environment and your health.

2.6 Do I Need to Mulch?

Mulching is giving your garden a cozy blanket that not only keeps it warm but also nurtures it. The benefits of mulching extend beyond just beautifying your garden beds; it plays a crucial role in maintaining the health of your soil, conserving moisture, regulating temperature, and suppressing weeds. When you lay down mulch, you are essentially helping to create a more stable and nurturing environment for your plants to thrive in.

Firstly, mulch helps in retaining soil moisture by reducing evaporation. This is particularly beneficial during the hot summer months when the sun can quickly dry out the soil. By keeping the soil moist, mulch helps your plants stay hydrated and healthy. Additionally, mulch acts as an insulator for the soil, keeping it cooler in the summer and warmer in the winter. This temperature regulation is vital for the root development of plants, as extreme temperatures can inhibit growth or even kill delicate roots.

Another significant advantage of mulching is its ability to suppress weeds. Weeds are not just unsightly; they compete with your plants for water, nutrients, and light. A layer of mulch blocks light from reaching the soil surface, preventing weed seeds from germinating. This natural weed control method reduces the need for chemical herbicides, making your garden safer and more environmentally friendly.

When it comes to choosing the right type of mulch, you have two main categories to consider: organic and inorganic. Organic mulches, such as wood chips, straw, leaves, or grass clippings, are beneficial because they decompose over time, adding valuable organic matter and nutrients back into the soil. This process also encourages the activity of beneficial soil organisms, which help to break down organic matter and maintain soil health. Inorganic mulches, such as stones, rubber chips, or landscape fabric, do not provide nutrients to the soil but are more durable and can be particularly useful in certain landscaping situations where longevity is desired.

Applying mulch to your garden is a straightforward process, but it requires some technique to maximize its benefits. The ideal time to mulch is in late spring, after the soil has warmed up. Applying mulch too early can slow the warming process, which can affect plant growth. Start by spreading a 2-4 inch layer of mulch around your plants, taking care to keep the mulch a few inches away from plant stems to prevent moisture buildup, which can lead to rot. For container gardens, a thinner layer of mulch, about 1-2 inches, is sufficient to provide the benefits without overwhelming the smaller soil volume.

Common mulching mistakes can sometimes lead to more harm than good. One such mistake is piling mulch too high against plant stems, often referred to as "volcano mulching." This practice can cause moisture to accumulate around the stem, leading to diseases and pest problems. Another mistake is using uncomposted wood chips or other organic materials that can rob the soil of nitrogen as they decompose. To avoid this, ensure that any organic mulch you use is well-composted before applying it to your garden. Lastly, be mindful of the source of your mulch. Some mulches, especially those that are free or low-cost, can contain weed seeds or be contaminated with pesticides, which can introduce problems to your garden.

The need to mulch is often thought of as something for large areas, around tree bases, or under bushes. Not using mulch in small areas, especially during the hot summer months or when plants are still establishing their root systems, can make the difference between those that thrive with the increased sunlight and those that wilt and potentially die.

Incorporating mulching into your gardening practice is a simple yet effective way to enhance the health of your plants and soil, conserve water, and naturally suppress weeds. With the right type and proper application technique, mulch can serve as an invaluable ally in creating a vibrant and sustainable garden. By understanding and implementing these mulching practices, you're not just decorating your garden— you're investing in its future health and productivity.

2.7 Do I Need to Fertilize?

Fertilizing your garden can sometimes feel like a delicate dance, trying to provide just the right nutrients at just the right time to help your plants flourish. Think of fertilizer as a supplement that assists in strengthening your plants, especially during critical phases of their growth. It's not always necessary, but when used correctly, it can significantly enhance the health and yield of your garden. Let's explore the best practices for fertilizer application, delve into natural fertilizers, and even touch on making your own, ensuring you feel confident and ready to nurture your garden in the most sustainable way.

Timing is everything when it comes to fertilizing. The goal is to support your plants during their most active growth phases. For most annuals and vegetables, this means applying a balanced fertilizer shortly after planting and again as they enter a phase of rapid growth, typically just as they begin to bloom. This helps ensure they have the nutrients they need to produce blooms and, eventually, fruit. Perennials, on the other hand, benefit from fertilization in the early spring as they exit dormancy and again in the fall to help them prepare for the winter. It's crucial to avoid over-fertilizing, which can lead to lush leaf growth at the expense of flowers and fruits and can even harm the plant's health, making it more susceptible to diseases and pests.

When choosing a fertilizer, consider opting for natural options which are better for your garden and the environment. Compost tea, manure, and bone meal are all excellent choices that provide essential nutrients and improve soil health. Compost tea is liquid gold for gardeners, made by steeping finished compost in water to create a nutrient-rich solution that can be applied directly to the soil or used as a foliar spray. Manure, whether from cows, horses, or chickens, is rich in nitrogen, phosphorus, and potassium, but it should be well-composted before use to avoid burning plants and to ensure pathogens are destroyed. Bone meal is a great source of phosphorus and calcium, ideal for promoting strong root development and flowering.

For those who love a DIY approach, making your own fertilizers can be a rewarding endeavor. One simple recipe is to blend used coffee grounds with eggshells and banana peels. Dry the ingredients, grind them into a fine powder, and sprinkle it around your plants. This mixture provides a gentle supply of nitrogen, potassium, and calcium. Another easy recipe involves soaking seaweed in a bucket of water for a few weeks and then using the water as a liquid fertilizer. Seaweed is rich in trace minerals and hormones that promote plant health and disease resistance.

The environmental impact of using natural fertilizers cannot be overstated. Unlike synthetic fertilizers, which are often high in salts and can leach into waterways, causing pollution and harming wildlife, natural fertilizers are gentle on the earth. They release nutrients slowly, which means less frequent application and minimal risk of runoff. Moreover, by using products such as compost tea or homemade blends, you're recycling waste products that might otherwise end up in a landfill, turning them into something that benefits your garden and contributes to a healthier planet.

Incorporating natural fertilizers into your gardening practice is a step toward creating a more sustainable and productive garden. Whether you choose to buy natural products or make your own, the key is to use them thoughtfully and responsibly, always considering the specific needs of your plants and the overall health of your garden ecosystem.

2.8 What Do I Do About Pests?

When it comes to maintaining a thriving garden, dealing with pests is an inevitable part of the adventure. However, with the right strategies in place, you can manage these uninvited guests effectively without resorting to harsh chemicals that might harm your garden's ecosystem or your own health. Let's explore several proactive steps you can take to prevent and control pest infestations.

Preventive Strategies

The best defense against pests is a good offense. By adopting cultural, mechanical, and biological strategies, you can prevent many pest issues before they start. Cultural practices involve maintaining a healthy garden through proper watering, fertilizing, and spacing of plants, which naturally reduces the likelihood of pest infestations. For example, overcrowded plants can create a humid microclimate that many pests find irresistible. Spacing your plants properly ensures adequate air circulation, which helps keep the foliage dry and less attractive to pests.

Mechanical controls are physical methods of preventing or removing pests from your garden. This includes actions like installing barriers or traps. Row covers made of lightweight fabric can be draped over plants to protect them from flying insects and birds without blocking light or rain. Similarly, collars made from cardboard or plastic placed around the base of young plants can deter cutworms, which are notorious for slicing through tender stems.

I use wire cloches over my lettuce because the bunnies love them as much as I do. Wire trash barrels can be an inexpensive substitute for ones that are sold specifically for gardeners or build your own with chicken wire. Cloches can be made from plastic bottles, big or small, and can serve as a protective environment from pests as well as from the elements, especially for seedlings which may benefit from a little assistance as they establish themselves.

Biological control involves using nature's own checks and balances to manage pests. This includes introducing or encouraging beneficial insects that prey on harmful pests. Ladybugs, lacewings, and predatory wasps are allies in the garden, feeding on aphids, caterpillars, and other pests that can damage your plants. Planting a diversity of species that flower at different times can help attract these beneficial insects, providing them with the nectar and pollen they need to thrive in your garden.

Pest Identification

Figure 9 *Aphid, Slug, and Japanese beetle*

Knowing your enemy is crucial in managing garden pests effectively. Spend time in your garden observing your plants and looking for signs of pest activity. Common pests as in aphids, slugs, and Japanese beetles are relatively easy to identify by the damage they cause. Aphids, for example, are small, soft-bodied insects that cluster on the undersides of leaves, sucking sap and cause leaves to curl and distort. Slugs leave shiny trails on the soil and chew large, irregular holes in leaves. Recognizing these signs early can help you take prompt action to mitigate damage.

Educational resources such as online databases, garden centers, and local extension services can be invaluable in helping you identify pests and understand their life cycles and behaviors. This knowledge is crucial in choosing the most effective and timely control methods.

Natural Remedies

When pests do make their way into your garden, natural remedies can be effective tools for keeping them at bay. One simple but effective remedy is a spray made from water and a few drops of mild dish soap. This soap spray can be used to treat infestations of aphids, mites, and whiteflies by breaking down the insects' waxy exterior, leading to dehydration. For a stronger impact, adding neem oil to the mix can help control harder-to-manage pests by disrupting their hormonal systems, making it harder for them to grow and lay eggs.

Another home remedy involves the use of garlic and hot pepper sprays, which act as potent repellents for many pests. To make this spray, blend a couple of hot peppers and a bulb of garlic with a pint of water, then strain the mixture and spray it directly on the affected plants. The strong odors and flavors are repulsive to many pests, keeping them at bay without harming your plants.

Homemade Organic Pesticides

For those who prefer to make their own pest controls, there are several recipes for organic pesticides that can be easily crafted from household ingredients. One effective recipe is a baking soda and oil mixture, which works well against fungal diseases and some insect pests. Mix a tablespoon of baking soda with a tablespoon of vegetable oil and a gallon of water. Spray this solution on the foliage of affected plants to help control fungal spores and provide a barrier against insect pests.

Encouraging natural predators in your garden is another environmentally friendly strategy to reduce pest populations. Creating a habitat that attracts birds, frogs, and beneficial insects can help keep pest numbers in check. This can be as simple as installing a bird feeder or a small pond, or letting a part of your garden grow a little wilder to provide shelter for these helpful creatures.

By integrating these preventive and natural strategies into your garden care routine, you can manage pests effectively without relying on chemical pesticides.

2.9 How Do I Get Rid of and Prevent Weeds?

Managing weeds in your garden can sometimes feel as though you're playing a never-ending game of whack-a-mole. Just when you think you've got them under control, new weeds seem to pop up overnight. But fear not! With some proactive strategies and a bit of elbow grease, you can maintain a weed-free garden that allows your plants to thrive without competition. Stay tuned for some effective ways to prevent weed germination, remove existing weeds safely, and use organic methods to keep them at bay.

Preventative Measures

Again the key to effective management is prevention. One of the most effective preventative measures you can take is to create a physical barrier that stops weeds before they start. Landscape fabric, often used under mulch, can be a gardener's best friend. This fabric acts as a block, preventing weed seeds from reaching the soil and germinating, while still allowing water and air to reach the roots of your desired plants. When laying down landscape fabric, ensure it covers the entire area and overlaps at the seams to prevent any light from reaching potential weeds. Secure the fabric with garden staples to keep it in place, and then cover it with a layer of mulch or gravel for added protection and aesthetics. Consider using cardboard in place of landscape fabric as a weed barrier to keep costs down and as a recycling option.

Another preventative strategy is to use the "crowding out" method by planting densely. When you plant your flowers and vegetables close together, they naturally shade the soil, keeping it cool and making it less inviting for weed seeds to sprout. This method helps in weed prevention and maximizes your garden's productivity by using space efficiently.

Physical Removal

Despite your best efforts at prevention, some weeds will inevitably find their way into your garden. When they do, physical removal is often the most immediate and effective method to keep them under control. The key here is timing; removing weeds before they mature and go to seed will greatly reduce future populations. For young weeds, hand-pulling can be very effective, especially after a rain when the soil is moist and roots come out more easily. For larger or more stubborn weeds, tools such as a hoe or a weeder can help you remove them root and all without too much strain.

It's important to be thorough when removing weeds by hand. Make sure to get as much of the root system as possible, as many weeds can regenerate from root fragments left in the soil. It's extremely satisfying when you're able to remove a weed with its entire root and to know that you "whacked" the mole! Dispose of the weeds away from your garden area to prevent any seeds from finding their way back into your soil. Regularly walking through your garden and removing weeds as soon as you spot them can keep this task manageable and prevent overwhelming infestations.

Organic Mulches

Utilizing organic mulches not only helps retain soil moisture and regulate temperature but is also an excellent way to suppress weeds. Organic mulches, such as wood chips, straw, or leaves, provide a physical barrier that blocks light from reaching the soil surface, thus preventing weed seed germination. As these mulches decompose, they also contribute organic matter to the soil, enhancing its structure and fertility, which benefits your plants. Apply a layer of organic mulch about 2-3 inches thick around your plants. Be sure not to pile it too close to the stems to avoid moisture-related issues like rot.

Additionally, some types of organic mulch, such as cedar bark, have natural oils that act as weed repellents, offering double-duty benefits for your garden. Refreshing the mulch layer annually, or as needed when it begins to thin, can help maintain its effectiveness against weeds and keep your garden looking tidy.

Natural Herbicides

For those times when physical removal isn't practical, natural herbicides can be a useful tool in your weed-control arsenal. Vinegar, for example, is a powerful organic herbicide that can kill weeds on contact. The acetic acid in vinegar desiccates the plant's leaves on contact, causing them to dry out and die. To use vinegar as a weed killer, simply spray it directly onto the weeds on a sunny day. Be careful to target only the weeds, as vinegar can harm your desirable plants as well.

Another natural herbicide is boiling water, which can be poured directly onto the weed plants. This method is especially effective for weeds growing in cracks in sidewalks or driveways, where it's difficult to use other removal methods. Boiling water works by scalding the plant and root tissues, causing immediate and effective weed control.

By incorporating these strategies into your gardening routine, you can maintain a more weed-free environment that allows your plants to thrive without the competition for nutrients, water, and light. Consistency is key in weed management, and a little effort goes a long way in keeping your garden healthy and beautiful.

2.10 What is Pruning and Do I Have to Do It?

Pruning might seem like just another chore in the garden, but it's actually a vital practice that can significantly enhance the health and productivity of your plants. When you prune, you're cutting back branches and leaves and strategically shaping your plants to optimize their growth and fruit production. It's about making thoughtful cuts that help your plants thrive.

Pruning Benefits

The benefits of pruning are numerous. Firstly, it helps to improve the health of your plants by removing dead or diseased branches, which can be breeding grounds for pests and pathogens. By cutting these away, you prevent potential problems from spreading to the rest of the plant or even to neighboring plants in your garden. Pruning also encourages air circulation, which reduces the damp conditions that many diseases thrive in.

Another significant benefit of pruning is that it enhances the productivity of fruit-bearing plants. By removing some of the branches, you allow more light to reach the interior of the plant, which is crucial for the development of fruit. Additionally, by thinning out some of the fruiting branches, you ensure that the plant's energy is concentrated on producing fewer, but larger and higher-quality fruits. This technique, known as selective thinning, can make a world of difference in the yield and quality of your harvest. Use this on your tomato plants, preserving the main branches that produce flowers, and eliminating the side branches and witness the increase in your tomato crop.

Pruning is not just about health and productivity; it's also an essential tool for shaping the aesthetic of your garden. Whether you're looking to maintain a particular size or shape for your plants, or you want to encourage a certain form, pruning gives you the control to sculpt your garden's appearance. Regular pruning ensures that your plants look tidy and well-maintained, contributing to the overall charm and design of your gardening space.

Pruning Techniques

There are several techniques you can use, depending on what your plants need. One common method is called deadheading, which involves removing spent flowers to encourage plants to produce more blooms. This technique is particularly useful for flowering plants like roses or geraniums, where continuous blooming is desirable.

Another technique is selective pruning, where you remove specific branches to shape the plant's growth or to improve its structure. This might involve thinning out crowded areas to enhance air circulation or cutting back overgrown branches to maintain a plant's size and shape. When making cuts, always use sharp, clean pruning tools to make clean cuts that heal quickly, and always cut just above a bud that faces the direction you want the new branch to grow. This encourages the plant to grow in a specific direction, helping you control its shape and structure.

Timing for Pruning

Timing your pruning is crucial for getting the best results. Most deciduous trees and shrubs are best pruned in late winter or early spring before new growth begins. This timing allows you to see the structure of the plant clearly without the leaves in the way, making it easier to decide which branches to remove. It also means that the wounds heal quickly in the spring growth, reducing the risk of disease.

For flowering plants, the timing of pruning depends on when they bloom. Plants that flower in early spring, such as forsythia and azaleas, should be pruned immediately after they finish blooming. This is because these plants set their flower buds during the previous year, and pruning them in winter or early spring would remove the buds and reduce flowering. Summer-flowering plants, like roses and hydrangeas, can be pruned in late winter or early spring because they develop buds on new growth.

Tools for Pruning

Having the right tools for pruning can make the task easier and more effective. The basic tools you'll need include a pair of sharp hand pruning shears for cutting thin branches and stems, loppers for thicker branches, and a pruning saw for the thickest branches. Keeping these tools clean and sharp ensures they make clean cuts that heal quickly, preventing damage to your plants.

Caring for your pruning tools is also essential. Regularly clean the blades with soapy water and dry them thoroughly to prevent rust. Sharpen the blades as needed to keep them cutting smoothly, and oil the moving parts to keep them working well. Store your tools in a dry, clean place to protect them from the elements and to keep them ready for the next pruning session.

Pruning is a vital practice that enhances the health, productivity, and beauty of your garden. By understanding the benefits and techniques of pruning, and by doing it at the right time with the right tools, you can keep your garden looking its best and producing abundantly. With these skills, you're well-equipped to take your gardening to the next level.

2.11 Wrapping Up Chapter 2

In this chapter, we've explored the essentials of effective gardening, from choosing the right tools to understanding the intricacies of soil management and pest control. As you move forward, remember that each plant in your garden has its unique needs and responses to care. The techniques and strategies discussed here provide a foundation for you to build upon as you continue to learn and grow as a gardener. Next, we will delve into the challenges gardeners face and how to overcome them. You are not alone in this quest and together we will face them head on.

Help Make Raised Bed and Container Gardening Accessible to Everyone

Gardening can be such a joy, and I want to spread that happiness to everyone. That's why I wrote *The Practical Guide to Raised Bed and Container Gardening* – to help you and others grow beautiful gardens easily.

Now, I need your help...

Would you help someone just starting their gardening journey? Someone who is excited but unsure where to begin?

My goal is to make gardening easy, fun, and accessible for everyone, and your review can make that happen. When people see good reviews, they feel more confident that this book can help them.

So, here's my favor to ask:

Please leave a review for *The Practical Guide to Raised Bed and Container Gardening.*

Your review costs nothing and takes less than a minute, but it can make a big difference. It can help...

- A new gardener start their first garden with confidence.
- A family grow their own fresh vegetables.
- A community come together over a shared love of plants.

- A person find a new hobby that brings them happiness.
- Someone's dream of a beautiful garden come true.

To help, simply scan the QR code to leave your review:

By leaving a review, you're helping another gardener just like you. You're part of a caring community that loves to share and grow together.

Thank you so much for your support. I'm excited to help you grow a fantastic garden, and I hope you love the tips and tricks in this book.

Happy gardening!

Your fellow gardening enthusiast,
GG Barre

PS - If you think this book will help someone you know, please share it with them. Goodwill and knowledge are gifts worth sharing.

THREE

Gardening Challenges

E very gardener, whether you're just starting out or have been tending plants for years, will face some challenges along the way. Think of these not as roadblocks, but as opportunities to grow and learn alongside your garden. This chapter delves into some of the most common issues you might encounter, armed with practical advice to help you navigate these hurdles with confidence and ease. Let's turn those potential pitfalls into stepping stones for gardening success!

3.1 What are Some Common Issues?

Identifying Nutrient Deficiencies

Plants, much as people, need a balanced diet to thrive. Nutrient deficiencies can manifest in various ways, making your once vibrant plants look a little under the weather.

Yellowing leaves, stunted growth, and poor flowering are just a few signs that your plants might be missing key nutrients. Nitrogen, phosphorus, and potassium are the big three essential nutrients, often referred to as N-P-K. If your plants have yellowing leaves, they might be craving more nitrogen. Weak stems and a purple tinge on leaves could suggest a phosphorus deficiency. A lack of potassium might show up as brown scorching and curling of leaf tips. Rectifying these deficiencies involves adjusting your soil amendments. Adding compost can often introduce the needed balance, but for more targeted remedies, a specific fertilizer—with organic options such as bone meal for phosphorus or greensand for potassium —might be necessary.

Watering Wisely

Watering seems straightforward, but finding the right balance can be tricky. Both underwatering and overwatering bring their challenges. Underwatered plants can wilt, have dry and brittle leaves, and fail to grow. Overwatered plants may have leaves that are soft and discolored, and too much water can lead to root rot. The key is checking the soil before watering. Stick your finger about an inch deep—if the soil feels dry, it's time to water; if it's damp, wait a bit longer. Consider the type of soil and adjust your watering schedule accordingly. Sandy soils dry out faster, while clay soils retain moisture longer. Using mulch can help maintain soil moisture and reduce the frequency of watering. For precise watering, drip irrigation systems can be a game-changer, delivering water directly to the roots where it's needed most.

Improving Soil Structure

The foundation of a healthy garden is good soil. Improving your garden's soil structure can greatly enhance plant health and ease other gardening challenges. If your soil is too sandy, it might drain too quickly and not retain nutrients well. Adding organic matter like compost or peat moss can help. If you're dealing with heavy clay soil, which drains poorly and can suffocate roots, incorporating coarse sand or gypsum can improve its texture. Regularly adding organic matter is beneficial for all soil types as it helps improve aeration, enhances drainage, and maintains moisture levels. A well-structured soil is like a cozy, well-stocked home for your plants, providing everything they need right where they need it.

Lighting Adjustments

Sunlight is the lifeblood of your garden. Too little light and your plants may struggle to grow and produce fruits or flowers; too much, and some plants can get scorched. If your garden isn't getting enough light, consider pruning nearby trees or shrubs to let more sunlight in. For potted plants, simply moving them to a brighter spot might do the trick. If too much sun is the issue, using shade cloths during the hottest parts of the day can protect sensitive plants. Understanding the specific light needs of your plants is crucial— while vegetables might relish six (6) to eight (8)hours of full sun, some perennials prefer the cooler, shadier spots.

Visualizing Success: Interactive Garden Mapping

To help you visualize and plan the optimal placement for your plants based on their nutrient and light needs, consider creating an interactive garden map. An interactive garden map is a digital tool that can be accessed on-line through several websites. This can be a fun and practical tool, allowing you to sketch out your garden space, play around with the locations of different plants, and note areas where you might need to adjust the soil or lighting. You can update and adjust this map throughout the seasons, making it a living document that grows and adapts as your garden does. This tool can also be an inviting way to get your kids or grandkids interested and involved in gardening.

Navigating these common gardening challenges might seem daunting at first, but with a bit of knowledge and the right tools, you'll find yourself growing not just a garden, but also your confidence and skills as a gardener. As you adjust watering schedules, tweak nutrient levels, or shift plants to catch the optimal light, each step brings you closer to the lush, flourishing garden you're dreaming of. Let's keep those green thumbs working, and remember, every challenge is just an opportunity in disguise!

3.2 What Do I Do If My Plants Look Sick?

When your plants start showing signs of distress, it can be a bit like noticing a loved one feeling under the weather. You know something's not quite right, but you might not know exactly what's wrong or how to help. Plant diseases can manifest in many ways—yellowing leaves, spots, stunted growth, or wilting are just a few symptoms that something might be amiss. Understanding what's affecting your plants is the first step to getting them back on track. Let's explore some common plant diseases, how to prevent them, and what natural treatments you can use to nurse your garden back to health.

Plant diseases often come in fungal, bacterial, or viral forms. Powdery mildew, a fungal disease, appears as a white or gray powdery coating on leaves, typically in late summer. It thrives in both very humid or very dry weather and can spread rapidly if not controlled. Blight, caused by fungi or bacteria, can lead to brown spots on leaves and fruit, eventually causing them to rot. Viruses, which are often spread by insects, can cause a variety of symptoms, including mosaic patterns on leaves, stunted growth, and malformed fruits. Each disease has its own telltale signs, and getting familiar with these can help you catch them early.

To prevent diseases, start with cultural practices that promote healthy growth. Rotating your crops each year is crucial; it prevents pathogens that may have settled in the soil from infecting the same plant family repeatedly. Good spacing between plants improves air circulation and reduces the humidity that many pathogens thrive on. Also, choosing disease-resistant plant varieties can dramatically reduce the prevalence of diseases in your garden. These varieties have been bred to resist specific pathogens and can be a lifesaver, especially in regions where certain diseases are common.

When it comes to treating plant diseases naturally, there are several effective options. Neem oil, a natural pesticide, has properties that can combat fungal infections and deter insects that transmit viruses. It's safe for use on vegetables and fruits and is biodegradable, making it an excellent choice for eco-conscious gardeners to use for strategic planning. For bacterial infections, a baking soda spray (a teaspoon of baking soda mixed with a quart of water) can create an alkaline environment on the leaf surface, which is inhospitable to many bacteria. Always test any homemade spray on a small area first to ensure it doesn't harm the plant.

Garden hygiene plays a pivotal role in disease prevention. Keeping your garden clean can significantly reduce the spread of pathogens. Remove and dispose of any diseased plant parts immediately; do not compost them as this can spread the disease to other parts of your garden. Regularly cleaning your garden tools, especially after working with diseased plants, prevents the spread of pathogens. A simple rinse with a bleach solution (one part bleach to nine parts water) can effectively disinfect tools. A clean garden is a healthy garden, and taking these proactive steps can keep your plants looking their best.

3.3 What Do I Do if My Plants Aren't Thriving?

When your plants aren't thriving despite your best efforts, it might feel like a mystery you're eager to solve. Often, the secret to revitalizing your garden lies beneath the surface in the soil itself. Recognizing the signs of nutrient deficiencies is crucial to getting your green friends back to their best health.

Let's explore how you can become a detective in your own garden, spotting these signs and taking action to correct them.

One of the first signs that your plants are lacking in nutrients might appear on their leaves. Yellow leaves can indicate a deficiency in nitrogen, a vital nutrient that affects the plant's ability to produce chlorophyll. If you notice purple or reddish hues on the undersides of leaves or along the veins, this could be a sign of phosphorus deficiency, particularly in cooler weather. Potassium deficiencies often manifest as browning or crisping on the edges of leaves. These symptoms give you clues about what your plants are missing, but remember, symptoms can sometimes overlap with other issues such as pests or diseases, so it's crucial to look at the overall health of the plant and its growing conditions for more accurate diagnosis.

Soil testing is a terrific tool that can provide a wealth of information about what's happening below the surface. Simple home testing kits are available at most garden centers and online retailers, and they can tell you the pH level of your soil as well as the primary nutrient levels. For a more detailed analysis, you can send a soil sample to a local extension service or a private lab. They can test for a wide range of elements, including micronutrients that are often overlooked but can be crucial for plant health. This detailed soil profile helps tailor your approach, ensuring you're not just throwing fertilizer at the problem but actually addressing the specific needs of your soil.

Once you've pinpointed the deficiencies, amending your soil is the next step. If nitrogen is low, incorporating organic matter such as compost, manure, or a nitrogen-rich plant meal can boost levels. For phosphorus deficiencies, bone meal or rock phosphate can be effective. Potassium levels can be increased with potash or a compost made from banana peels. Always integrate these amendments into the soil gently; disturbing the roots too much can stress your plants further. Additionally, consider the timing of these amendments. Some nutrients, like nitrogen, are best added as a quick-release source at planting or as a top dressing during the growth season, while others, like phosphorus, can be mixed into the soil pre-planting as they are slow to break down and become available to plants.

Maintaining soil health isn't just about reacting to problems. Adopting preventive measures can help you avoid nutrient deficiencies in the first place. Regularly adding organic matter to your soil can help maintain good nutrient levels and soil structure. Crop rotation is another beneficial practice; different plants use different amounts and types of nutrients, so rotating them helps prevent depleting any one nutrient from the soil. Also, consider using cover crops during the off-season. Plants like clover or alfalfa can fix nitrogen from the atmosphere and add it to the soil, enriching it for the next planting season. Other nitrogen-fixing plants include beans, peas and lupines.

In gardening, as in life, prevention is often easier than cure. By keeping an eye out for the early signs of trouble, testing your soil to understand its specific needs, and amending and maintaining it thoughtfully, you can keep your garden flourishing. This proactive approach saves you time and resources and also turns gardening into a more rewarding experience as you watch your plants grow strong and healthy.

3.4 Wrapping Up Chapter 3

In this chapter we've journeyed through the critical aspects of detecting and correcting issues in your garden that prevent your plants from thriving. From the tell-tale signs of nutrient deficiencies to the comprehensive strategies for soil testing and amendment, you're now equipped with the knowledge to ensure your garden remains a vibrant and productive space. Now, let's step into the next chapter where we'll explore the exciting world of harvest, helping you reap the rewards of your diligently cultivated garden.

FOUR

Harvest

Stepping into your garden and seeing the fruits of your labor ready to be picked is one of the most rewarding moments any gardener can experience. It's the culmination of weeks or months of nurturing, watering, and caring for your plants. But how do you know exactly when it's the right time to harvest? And once you do, what's the best way to gather your produce without harming the plants that have worked so hard to bear it? Let's dive into the art of harvesting, a critical step that ensures the fruits and vegetables you've tended with so much love and care are reaped at their peak of flavor and nutrition.

4.1 How Do I Know When Vegetables and Fruit are Ready to be Picked?

Timing Your Harvest

Determining the perfect time to harvest your crops can feel as though it's a mix of science and intuition. Each type of vegetable and fruit has its own signs that tell you it's ready to be picked, and knowing these can make the difference between a good harvest and a great one. Tomatoes, for example, should be harvested when they are uniformly colored and slightly soft to the touch. If you pick them too early, they won't have developed their full flavor; too late, and they might become mushy. Leafy greens like spinach and lettuce are best harvested in the morning when they are still crisp from the cool night air. Waiting until the afternoon when the sun has drawn out some of their moisture can result in a less crisp texture.

Root vegetables like carrots and radishes offer a little peek above the soil that can help judge their size, but the true test often requires a gentle probe into the soil to feel around the top of the root. If it feels substantial, it's likely ready to pull. For fruiting vegetables like cucumbers and squash, check for size and color. They should be firm and have a uniform color typical of ripe produce.

Since root vegetables are the most difficult to judge, it helps to keep track of when seeds or tubers were planted and to pay attention to seed packet labeling since harvest will vary based on variety. If vegetables are grown from seedlings, this timing will obviously be shorter. In general, the following rules of thumb apply for the most common of these root vegetables:

- Radishes typically take 25 to 30 days from seed to harvest. Roots should be about 1 inch in diameter.
- Carrots typically take 70 to 80 days from seed to harvest. Check root size by gently pulling back the soil around the tops.
- Potatoes typically take 70 to 120 days from planting of tubers to harvest. Potatoes can be harvested when foliage begins to yellow and die back.
- Sweet potatoes typically take 90 to 170 days from planting of slips to harvest. Harvest sweet potatoes when the leaves and vines start to turn yellow and die back.
- Turnips typically take 30 to 60 days from seed to harvest. Most varieties can be harvested when the roots are 2 to 3 inches in diameter. The greens can be harvested earlier, when they reach 4 to 6 inches in height.
- Beets typically take 50 to 70 days from seed to harvest. Harvest when the roots are about 1 to 3 inches in diameter. The greens can be harvested earlier, when they reach 4 to 6 inches in height.
- Parsnips typically take 120 to 180 days from seed to harvest. Harvest when roots are about 1 ½ to 2 inches in diameter. Taste improves after frost exposure and parsnips are often harvested late in the season after the first few frosts.

Timing is also influenced by what you plan to do with your harvest. If you're looking forward to eating your produce fresh, it's best to pick it close to when you'll use it for the best taste and nutritional value. However, if you plan to store or preserve your harvest, picking it at the peak of ripeness is crucial to ensure it holds up well during storage or the preservation process.

Harvesting Techniques

Once you've determined it's the right time to pick your produce, the next step is to harvest it in a way that ensures the ongoing health of your plant. The technique varies slightly by the type of plant and the part of the plant you are harvesting.

For fruits and vegetables that grow on vines or stems, such as tomatoes, peppers, or squash, use a sharp pair of garden shears or a knife to cut the fruit from the plant. Pulling or twisting them off can damage the plant and the fruit, and can create open wounds that are susceptible to pests or diseases. For leafy greens, you can either pick leaves individually, starting from the outermost part of the plant, or cut the whole plant off at its base. If you choose the latter method, leave about an inch of the stem in the ground; often, it will sprout new leaves for a second harvest.

Root vegetables require a gentle touch to avoid breaking the roots. Loosen the soil around the plant with a garden fork or a spade, then pull the vegetable by the base of its greens. Shake off any excess soil and, if not using immediately, leave the dirt on as it helps in storage.

By understanding the right time to harvest and employing the correct techniques, you ensure the best quality of your garden produce and encourage healthy growth for continued yields. As you gather your bounty, remember that each vegetable or fruit you place in your basket is a testament to your dedication and care—congratulate yourself...and no, taking selfies with your harvest is not weird!

4.2 How Do I Plan for Year-Round Harvests?

Planning for a year-round harvest transforms gardening from a seasonal hobby into a continual source of food and enjoyment. It begins with understanding the concept of crop rotation. Rotating your crops annually is a tried-and-true method that helps maintain soil health and reduce pest problems. Instead of planting the same crop in the same spot each year, rotate them through different areas of your garden. This method prevents certain soil-borne diseases from taking hold and reduces the depletion of specific nutrients. For instance, legumes, like beans and peas, fix nitrogen in the soil, which can be beneficial for following crops that consume more nitrogen, such as leafy greens.

Succession planting is another strategy that maximizes the productivity of your garden. By planning the planting of new seeds at intervals, you can ensure a continuous supply of produce at different times throughout the growing season. For example, you could plant radishes or lettuce, which mature quickly, alongside carrots that take longer to reach harvest time. Once you harvest the radishes and lettuce, you have space to plant another crop (or more radishes and lettuce), if the season allows. This staggered approach extends your harvest and helps manage the workload, making it easier to maintain your garden without feeling overwhelmed. It keeps your garden productive and your kitchen stocked with fresh produce from early spring through late fall.

Choosing the right crops for each season is crucial for a year-round harvest. Each climate zone has specific planting windows for various vegetables. In spring, focus on cool-weather crops like lettuce, spinach, and peas, which can tolerate the mild frosts of early season. As the weather warms, transition to heat-loving plants like tomatoes, peppers, and cucumbers. For fall, plant crops that can withstand cooler temperatures, such as kale, broccoli, and carrots. Many of these can survive early frosts, especially if provided with some protection, such as a layer of mulch. Refer to the tables in **Section 1.10 What are Climate (Hardiness) Zones and Why are They Important?** above for examples of vegetables, flowers, and fruit that can be planted in the various climate zones throughout the various seasons.

Winter doesn't have to mean the end of your gardening. In colder climates, gardening can continue with the help of structures like cold frames and greenhouses. Cold frames, simple structures with a transparent top that captures sunlight and insulates plants, can be easily built. Start with a bottomless box made of weather-resistant wood or recycled materials, positioning the frame so it faces south. Cover the top with a clear lid, often an old window or a custom piece of polycarbonate. This setup allows you to grow cold-hardy vegetables like spinach and lettuce even when the temperatures drop.

For those who prefer something larger, building a DIY green-house might be the answer. Begin with a sturdy frame of PVC pipes or wood, and cover it with a clear, durable material like polycarbonate sheets. Ensure your greenhouse has ventilation to regulate temperature and humidity on warmer days. A greenhouse extends your growing season and also houses a wider variety of plants, including those typically grown in much warmer climates.

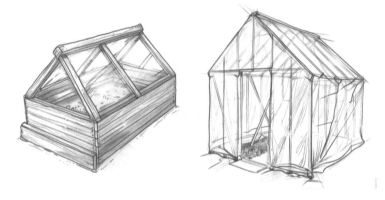

Figure 10 Example Cold Frame and Greenhouse

If building isn't your thing, cold frames and greenhouses can also be purchased. They come in various sizes and materials, fitting different budgets and space constraints. A simple online search or a visit to your local garden center can provide options that fit your needs. When choosing, consider the size of your garden, the typical weather conditions in your area, and how much you're willing to invest.

Grow lights can provide the necessary light spectrum and intensity that plants need for photosynthesis regardless of outdoor conditions. Blue light promotes growth, red light encourages flowering and fruiting, and full-spectrum light mimics natural sunlight. The intensity of these lights can be adjusted depending upon the needs of different plants, with higher intensity typically needed for plants during active growth and flowering stages. These lights can be set on a timer to provide the right amount and intensity of light when natural sunlight is unavailable. For outdoor plants, the growing season can be extended by starting seeds indoors before the last frost and then transplanting them once the danger of frost has passed.

4.3 Wrapping Up Chapter 4

In this chapter we discussed harvesting and how we can implement a year-round harvest. Strategies such as crop rotation, succession planting, choosing season-appropriate crops, and extending the growing season with cold frames, greenhouses, or grow lights can ensure enjoyment of the benefits of gardening any day of the year. This continuous cycle can provide your family with fresh produce year-round.

FIVE

Reflection and Looking Forward

As you take a moment to glance back at the soil tilled and seeds sown both literally and metaphorically, it's clear that every little effort in gardening, much as life's endeavors, weaves a unique story. Each leaf, blossom, and fruit holds a narrative of patience, learning, and growth. This chapter is a celebration of your story, a reflection on the journey from sprouting seeds to blooming gardens, and an exploration of how these green spaces tie communities together, fostering personal and collective growth.

5.1 Your Success Story: From Beginner to Green Thumb

Inspiring Journeys

Remember the first time you planted a seed. The uncertainty mixed with excitement—a microcosm of life's own ebb and flow. Now, picture that experience magnified through the journeys of countless others who started with little more than a patch of soil and a dream.

In the introduction, you learned how I have killed almost every house plant I've ever possessed, even cacti. When I lived in a house with more than enough space for an outdoor garden, I was intimidated by even attempting to start such an endeavor. Finally, when I moved into my apartment with a community garden, I figured I'd give gardening another shot. As a kid in Hawaii, it was easy to grow vegetables with mom, given the warm temperatures, more than adequate rainfall, and mom's encouragement. But I didn't think I could duplicate this anywhere else and at any other time. Imagine my surprise when I was growing my own vegetables in my first year in the community garden--oh, how proud I was! And yes, I shared pictures of my harvest on social media, and it felt great!! It just goes to show that gardening really is and can be rewarding for everyone.

Take this moment to celebrate what you attempted and succeeded in accomplishing! It may not have yielded as much as you were hoping for, but you put yourself out there and made the effort. From what you've learned, you will undoubtedly improve over time--you should be very proud of yourself!! Perhaps you got more than you were expecting and what a wonderful surprise—keep up the good work!

There are so many stories of triumph on social media and in your communities, whether apartment buildings or suburban homesteads. If you ever need reassurance or inspiration, take a moment to see what others have accomplished or post your own accomplishments. It can be just the help someone else needs who may be unsure, struggling, or wanting to give up. Again, stay the course, and you will be rewarded!

Lessons Learned

Each gardening story is rich with lessons learned along the way—both successes and setbacks that enrich the gardener's knowledge and skills. In my first year in my community garden, I had no idea what I was doing and literally copied the actions of my gardening neighbors. Every year has brought me more confidence, and I'm certain that confidence will bloom in you too. Setbacks are normal, as in every other aspect of life, but they give us another data point that we can use when we need to fall back on all we've learned.

Community Impact

Gardens often start as personal sanctuaries but they seldom remain solitary. They have a profound way of growing tendrils into the community, creating spaces for connection and shared experiences. Consider a community garden in a small suburban neighborhood (that's me!), where each plot tells a different story and contributes to a tapestry of communal cohesion. Here, experienced gardeners share seeds with novices, knowledge is exchanged over garden fences, and harvests are celebrated together. Such spaces become more than just places to grow food; they are vital social hubs that foster relationships and strengthen community bonds. The community garden is where I've met the few people I know in my apartment complex.

Personal Growth

Reflecting on the personal growth that accompanies gardening, it is evident that each season brings its own set of challenges and triumphs. Gardening teaches resilience, as the gardener learns to adapt to unforeseen challenges like pests or unpredictable weather. It nurtures a sense of responsibility—from the commitment to regular watering and weeding to the stewardship of the land and its resources. Most profoundly, gardening can be a meditative practice, a way to reconnect with oneself and the rhythms of nature. There is definitely something powerful in touching the earth and literally getting your hands dirty. For me, gardening is my opportunity to get outside in the fresh air and clear my mind as I concentrate on caring for my plants. Caring for living things fosters empathy and produces excitement and pride in seeing them grow. After spending time in my garden I find I sleep better at night and can come back to my desk job with new insight and energy. Give it a little time, and you'll be amazed at how much your garden can do for you!

Visual Element: Interactive Garden Journal

To help capture your growth and reflections through your gardening journey, consider maintaining an interactive garden journal. This tool can be a place to note what you've planted, track your garden's progress, jot down what's thriving or struggling, and record how your garden makes you feel throughout the seasons. This practice helps in planning and improving your garden year after year and serves as a reflective space to witness your own growth as a gardener and as an individual.

As we reflect, we constantly use this information to guide us forward. The next section reminds us of the general seasonal activities we need to plan for in the coming year.

5.2 What Activities Do I Do During Which Season of the Year?

Gardening is not just a hobby; it's a year-round commitment that changes with the seasons. But don't let this scare you-- not everything needs to be done at the same time. Each period of the year brings its own set of tasks that help prepare your garden for the next phase of growth. Let's walk through what your gardening calendar should look like, from the fresh beginnings of spring to the deep dormancy of winter.

Spring Preparation

Spring is a season of awakening and renewal, not just for nature but for your garden too. It's a busy time filled with promise and preparation. Start by clearing out your garden beds or containers from any debris or remnants of last season's plants. This cleanup includes removing any weeds that have taken hold, as these unwanted guests can compete with your plants for nutrients and space.

It can also be a good time to start seedlings from seed indoors with the help of grow lights. **Section 6 Plant Profiles** provides seed germination times for common vegetables, flowers, and fruit. Germination times can vary based on temperature, humidity, and seed quality, so use these times to estimate when to start seeds so that the resultant seedlings are ready to be planted outdoors, as applicable, when the time is right.

Next, focus on the soil—your garden's foundation. Over the winter, soil can become compacted and depleted of nutrients. Begin by gently turning the soil in your raised beds or refreshing the soil in your containers. This aeration helps to improve drainage and oxygen flow to plant roots. Adding compost or a balanced organic fertilizer at this stage provides a boost of nutrients that will support plant growth throughout the season. If you're using raised beds, check the structure for any needed repairs or modifications. For container gardeners, make sure your pots are in good condition and have adequate drainage holes to prevent waterlogged soil.

Planting during spring varies depending on your local climate and the last expected frost dates. Hardy vegetables such as peas, spinach, and kale can be planted early, even before the last frost, as they can tolerate cooler temperatures. For warm-season crops like tomatoes, peppers, and most annual flowers, it's safest to wait until the danger of frost has passed. This is also a great time to plan your garden's layout, considering factors like sun exposure, plant height, and compatibility (remember those companion planting tips).

Summer Maintenance

As the weather warms up, your garden enters its most active growth phase, which means your maintenance tasks will shift towards supporting this vigorous development. Regular watering becomes crucial, especially for container gardens, which dry out faster than in-ground beds. Implementing a consistent watering schedule early in the morning helps to reduce evaporation and provides plants with enough moisture to withstand the heat of the day.

Monitoring soil health throughout the summer is key. Mulching around your plants with organic material like straw or wood chips can help retain moisture, suppress weeds, and keep the soil cool. Additionally, a mid-season application of compost or a gentle fertilizer can give plants a necessary nutrient boost during peak growing times.

Pests and diseases also tend to pop up more frequently in summer. Keep an eye on your plants for signs of distress, such as discolored leaves or stunted growth. Early detection is crucial for managing issues before they become severe. Natural remedies, like neem oil for pests or pruning out diseased areas, are often sufficient for treatment without resorting to harsh chemicals.

Summer to Fall Transition

As summer winds down, your garden needs help adjusting to the cooler days of fall. This transition period is a good time to start planting fall crops such as carrots, beets, and lettuce, which can benefit from the milder temperatures. Not that these vegetables can't also be planted in the spring and summer! It's also an excellent time to harvest summer crops at their peak to savor in your meals or preserve for later use.

Begin scaling back on watering as the temperatures drop and plants require less moisture. This adjustment helps plants harden off and prepares them for cooler weather. Continue to monitor for pests and diseases and manage them as needed. Removing any fallen leaves or spent plant matter can help prevent the spread of fungal diseases and keep your garden tidy.

Fall and Winter Care

Fall is the time to prepare your garden for the colder months ahead. If you're in a region where the ground freezes, it's crucial to protect your soil and perennial plants. Adding a layer of mulch after the first hard freeze can help insulate the soil, protecting roots from temperature fluctuations and retaining moisture during dry winter months.

For raised beds and container gardens, assess if any soil needs to be replenished or if containers need to be moved to a sheltered location to prevent cracking. Fall is also a great time to plant bulbs such as tulips and daffodils, which require a winter chilling period before they bloom in spring.

Winterizing Your Garden

Winter might appear to be a downtime for gardeners, but a few key tasks can greatly enhance your garden's success come spring. Protecting your soil is paramount. Cover your raised beds with a layer of organic material, such as leaves or straw, or consider planting a cover crop such as clover, which can be turned into the soil as green manure in the spring.

For container gardens, ensure that pots are protected from freezing conditions, either by wrapping them in insulating material or moving them indoors if possible. This protection prevents the soil from freezing completely, which can damage plant roots and crack containers.

As the garden rests under the winter sky, take time to plan and dream about the next growing season. This quiet period is perfect for ordering seeds, reading up on new gardening techniques, and perhaps sketching out new plans for your garden layout. Embrace this slower pace as a necessary season of rest, both for you and your garden, before the cycle begins anew with the next spring's thaw.

5.3 Planning for the Next Year

As the seasons change and your garden begins to settle under the weight of its own harvest, the time ripens for reflection and thoughtful preparation for the months ahead. One of the most rewarding aspects of gardening is the cyclical opportunity it presents to apply the lessons learned from the past season to the next. Each year, your garden's needs, along with your skills and understanding, evolve, offering a fresh canvas to refine your approach and enhance your garden's productivity and beauty.

Planning for the next season starts with a careful review of what worked and what didn't. This might mean noting which plants thrived and which struggled, or observing how changes in your gardening practice impacted your garden's overall health. Was there a particular area where the soil seemed too compacted or perhaps another where plants consistently performed well? These observations are invaluable as they guide what you might want to adjust in the coming year, be it crop rotation to prevent soil depletion or altering the position of your garden beds to optimize sunlight exposure.

A crucial aspect of this end-of-season reflection involves testing and amending your soil. Over a season, plants extract various nutrients from the soil, potentially leaving it less fertile for the following year. Taking the time to test your soil can reveal a lot about its condition—its pH level, nutrient content, and organic matter. This data serves as a roadmap for amending your soil to ensure it provides the best possible environment for plant growth. Depending on the results, you might need to add organic compost to enrich the soil, lime to adjust the pH, or other specific nutrients that your plants have depleted during the previous season.

In addition to soil care, consider the seeds you'll plant next season. Seed saving, an ancient practice rich with both practicality and a profound connection to the gardening ancestors before us, allows you to carry forward the legacy of your strongest and most beloved plants. As your garden blooms and produces, identify the plants that are flourishing exceptionally well—those that are robust, productive, and resilient. Collecting seeds from these champions saves you the expense of purchasing new seeds and gradually cultivates a garden stock uniquely adapted to your local environment and personal taste.

The process of saving seeds varies slightly from plant to plant but generally involves allowing the seeds to fully mature on the plant before harvesting them. For many vegetables and flowers, this means waiting until the end of the season when fruits have ripened and pods have dried. Tomatoes, for instance, require a bit more effort as their seeds are best saved by fermenting the pulp to remove the gelatinous coating, which can inhibit germination. Once collected, clean the seeds thoroughly and dry them completely to prevent mold; then store them in a cool, dry place, labeled with the plant type and date of collection. This organizes your seeds for future planting and also preserves the genetic diversity of your garden, adapting over seasons to thrive in its specific conditions.

This thoughtful approach to wrapping up your garden not only sets the stage for future bounty but also deepens your connection to the very cycles of nature, reinforcing the rewards of patience and persistence. With each passing year, these cycles of growth, reflection, and renewal enrich your garden as well as your experience as a gardener, turning each season into an opportunity for new growth and discovery. As you pack away your garden tools for the winter, let your mind start to imagine the possibilities of the next spring, armed with new knowledge and inspired by the successes of the past year.

5.4 Where Do We Go From Here?

As you continue to nurture your garden, drawing from the rich experiences and new skills you've developed, you might find yourself wondering about the next steps in your gardening adventure. One of the most enriching paths forward is to connect with other gardeners. Whether it's finding local gardening groups or diving into the vast resources available online, engaging with a community can significantly enhance your gardening journey.

Finding and joining local gardening groups can be as rewarding as watching your first seeds sprout. These groups often consist of fellow gardening enthusiasts who share a passion for growing and a wealth of knowledge. Local gardening clubs often meet regularly to discuss everything from the basics of vegetable gardening to more advanced botanical concepts. These gatherings are not just about sharing knowledge; they're also about building friendships. To find these groups, check local community boards, visit your local library, or search online for gardening clubs in your area. You might also find flyers at your local garden center. Joining these groups can provide moral support, inspire new projects, and give you access to a collective wisdom that is invaluable, especially when tackling new challenges in your garden.

In today's digital age, online forums and social media groups also offer tremendous resources. Platforms like GardenWeb, Reddit gardening forums, or Facebook gardening groups can connect you with gardeners not just locally but around the world. These platforms are bustling with activity where members share their garden successes, troubleshoot issues, and provide encouragement. They are perfect for when you need quick advice or want to see what other gardeners are doing in different parts of the world. Participating in these online communities can be especially useful during the off-season when you're planning next year's garden or looking for new ideas.

Another fantastic way to enhance your gardening skills is by participating in workshops and classes. Many local gardens, nurseries, and even community colleges offer sessions ranging from one-time workshops to ongoing courses in horticulture. These classes can help you refine your techniques, learn about new advancements in gardening, and even delve into specific areas such as permaculture or landscape design. The hands-on experience, guided by experts, provides a learning opportunity that is hard to replicate through other means. Plus, these classes often provide a chance to try out new skills in a supportive environment.

Sharing your gardening experiences, both the triumphs and the setbacks, plays a crucial role in the learning process. By discussing what you've learned, you not only solidify your own knowledge but also help others overcome similar obstacles. Consider starting a garden blog, joining a community garden, or even inviting friends for a garden tour. Sharing can also take the form of contributing to plant and seed swaps, writing articles for gardening newsletters, or giving a talk at a local gardening event. Each act of sharing enriches the community's knowledge and weaves tighter bonds among its members.

5.5 Wrapping Up Chapter 5

This chapter underscored the importance of community in the gardening world. As you move forward, remember that gardening is not just about the plants you grow but also about the connections you cultivate along the way. Whether through face-to-face meetings or virtual networks, each interaction holds the potential to deepen your gardening practice and enrich your life. The paths are many, and each offers unique opportunities to grow not just gardens but also friendships and networks. As we conclude, carry with you the knowledge that wherever your gardening adventures lead, a community of fellow enthusiasts is just a conversation away.

SIX

Plant Profiles

This chapter contains some of the most common vegetables, herbs, flowers, and fruit beginners may choose to plant in their gardens. USDA Hardiness Zones are listed—reference Table 8 in Section 1.10 for comparable Canadian zones. In many cases, some varieties can grow outside of these listed zones, so always consult the seed packaging or local garden center expert. This will give you the most detailed information based on your chosen variety. We'll read about each plant's needs and characteristics, ensuring you're well-equipped to nurture them from seedling to harvest.

Keep in mind that several of the fruit trees that will normally grow to quite large sizes are available in dwarf forms and that just one tree will more practically fit in the spaces we have to work with. For these reasons they are included in our listing of plant profiles as fruit are a fantastic addition to any garden.

6.1 Vegetables

Growing your own vegetables is a worthy undertaking; it saves money and many are fast-growing so you can see the benefits of your labor quicker. It also allows you to choose the conditions in which your edibles are grown. Have fun choosing the ones which will grow the best in your garden, and be adventurous by choosing one or more that you may have never before tasted.

Artichokes (Cynara scolymus) Zones 7 to 11

Artichokes are a perennial vegetable that can be grown as an annual in cooler climates. Start seeds indoors about 8 weeks before the last frost and transplant them when they are about 8 to 10 inches tall. Seeds generally germinate within 10 to 20 days. Plant about 3 to 4 feet apart in a sunny, well-drained area. Artichokes require regular watering and a balanced fertilizer to produce large, tender buds. Harvest when the buds are tight and before the flowers start to open.

Arugula (Eruca vesicaria) Zones 3 to 11

Arugula is a peppery, leafy green that grows quickly and can be harvested as soon as 4 weeks after planting. Seeds germinate in typically 5 to 7 days. It prefers cool temperatures and can be planted in early spring or fall. Sow seeds directly in the garden about ¼ in deep, spacing them about 1 inch apart and thin to about 6 inches apart as they grow. Arugula likes well-drained soil and requires regular watering, especially during dry periods. Fertilize with a low-nitrogen, high-phosphorus fertilizer to promote leafy growth.

Asparagus (Asparagus officinalis) Zones 3 to 8

Asparagus is a perennial with its young shoots used as a spring vegetable and is known for its unique, tender texture and distinct flavor. They are typically grown from crowns (1-year-old root systems) or seeds. Germination time for seeds is usually around 21 to 28 days. Seeds can be started indoors 12 to 14 weeks before the last expected frost. Asparagus requires full sun and thrives in well-drained sandy soil. Harvest takes about 2 to 3 years from planting to first harvest, and shoots are harvested in early spring when they are 6 to 8 inches tall. Asparagus beds can produce for 15 to 20 years with proper care.

Beets (Beta vulgaris) Zones 2 to 10

Beets can be grown in both spring and fall for a double harvest. Germination time is typically 5 to 10 days (about 3 to 4 weeks from seed to seedlings) and should be placed about ½ in deep and spaced about 4 inches apart. They prefer cool temperatures and moist, fertile soil. Regular watering is necessary to develop tender and flavorful roots. A general-purpose fertilizer low in nitrogen can be applied midseason for best results.

Bell Peppers (Capsicum annuum) Zones 2 to 8 (annuals), Zones 9 to 11 (perennials)

Bell peppers like warm weather and should be started indoors about 8 to 10 weeks before the last frost. Germination is typically 7 to 14 days. Transplant them 18 to 24 inches apart in a sunny, well-draining area. They require consistent moisture and benefit from mulching to maintain soil temperature and moisture. Fertilize with a balanced feed high in phosphorus to promote strong root development. Bell peppers are great companions for onions and parsley but should be kept away from beans and brassicas (such as bok choy, broccoli, etc.—see below).

Bok Choy (Brassica rapa var. chinensis) Zones 2 to 11

Bok choy, also known as pak choi, is a quick-growing vegetable that can be harvested as early as 30 days after planting. For a fall harvest, it's best to sow seeds directly in the garden in early spring or late summer. Germination is typically 4 to 8 days. Space plants about 6 to 12 inches apart in a sunny spot with fertile, well-drained soil. Bok choy needs regular watering to keep the soil evenly moist. A light application of a balanced fertilizer can help ensure rapid growth.

Broccoli (Brassica oleracea var. italica) Zones 3 to 10

Broccoli is a cool-season crop that thrives in moderate temperatures. Start seeds indoors 6 to 8 weeks before the last frost or plant seeds directly in early spring, 2 to 4 weeks before the last expected frost date, or in late summer for a fall harvest. Germination time is typically 5 to 10 days. Space plants about 18 inches apart in a sunny spot with fertile, well-drained soil. Keep the soil consistently moist and mulch to retain moisture. Fertilize with a nitrogen-rich fertilizer to promote lush, healthy growth.

Brussel Sprouts (Brassica oleracea var. gemmifera) Zones 3 to 10

Brussels sprouts are a cool-season crop that requires a long growing season to mature. Plant seeds indoors 4 to 6 weeks before the last frost and transplant seedlings outdoors about 2 to 3 weeks before the last frost. Direct sowing is also possible, 4 months before the first fall frost. Seeds typically germinate in 5 to 10 days. Space plants about 18 to 24 inches apart to allow for adequate air circulation and growth. Brussels sprouts prefer full sun and fertile, well-drained soil rich in organic matter. Consistent moisture is crucial, especially during the growing season. Fertilize with a balanced fertilizer or one slightly higher in nitrogen to promote vigorous growth.

Cabbage (Brassica oleracea var. capitata) Zones 2 to 10

Cabbage is a hardy vegetable that grows best in cool tempera-tures and fertile soil. Start seeds indoors about 6 to 8 weeks before the last frost or sow directly in the garden 4 to 6 weeks before the last frost or in late summer for a fall harvest. Germination time is typically 5 to 8 days. Space plants about 12 to 24 inches apart, depending on the cabbage variety. Cabbage requires consistent moisture, especially as the heads begin to form. Fertilize with a balanced vegetable fertilizer to encourage vigorous growth.

Carrots (Daucus carota subsp. sativus) Zones 3 to 10

Carrots prefer cooler temperatures and can be grown in spring and fall. Germination is typically 10 to 21 days, and it takes about 3 to 4 weeks to grow from seed to seedlings. They should be sown directly into the garden as they do not take well to transplanting. Space them about 3 inches apart in sandy or loamy soil for best root development. Carrots require deep watering to encourage proper root growth, but be careful not to overwater. They are relatively low-maintenance regarding fertilization but appreciate a potassium boost.

Cauliflower (Brassica oleracea var. botrytis) Zones 2 to 11

Cauliflower requires a bit more care and attention than its relatives in the brassica family. It's best to start seeds indoors about 4 to 6 weeks before the last frost and transplant them 18 to 24 inches apart in rich, well-drained soil. Seeds generally take 7 to 14 days to germinate. Cauliflower needs consistent moisture to prevent the heads from splitting. Protect plants from extreme temperatures with shade cloth or floating row covers. Fertilize with a balanced fertilizer designed for vegetables.

Corn (Zea mays) Zones 3 to 11

Corn is a warm-season crop that should be planted after the last frost when the soil has warmed. Seeds generally take 7 to 10 days to germinate. Plant seeds about 1 inch deep and 4 to 6 inches apart in rows spaced 2 to 3 feet apart. Corn requires full sun and well-drained soil. It is a heavy feeder and benefits from a nitrogen-rich fertilizer applied at planting and again when the plants are knee-high. Corn requires regular watering, especially during pollination and ear development.

Cucumbers (Cucumis sativus) Zones 4 to 12

Cucumbers are a warm-season crop that can be grown on the ground or on a trellis. Seeds generally take 7 to 10 days to germinate. Plant seeds directly in the garden after the last frost when the soil has warmed. Space plants about 12 inches apart in a sunny, well-draining area. Cucumbers require regular watering, especially during flowering and fruit development. A balanced fertilizer applied at planting and again during the growing season can enhance growth and yield.

Eggplant (Solanum melongena) Zones 4 to 12

Eggplant is a warm-season crop that requires a long growing season. Start seeds indoors about 8 to 10 weeks before the last frost and transplant them 18 to 24 inches apart in a sunny, well-drained area. Seeds generally take 7 to 14 days to germinate. Eggplant prefers full sun and fertile, well-drained soil. It requires regular watering, especially during dry periods, and a balanced fertilizer to promote strong growth and fruit development.

Green Beans (Phaseolus vulgaris) Zones 3 to 10

Green beans are warm-season plants that should be planted after the last spring frost. Seeds generally take 7 to 10 days to germinate. They grow quickly, with seedlings ready in about 2 to 3 weeks, and can be harvested in about 50 to 60 days. Plant them about 6 inches apart. They need moderate watering, especially when flowering and developing pods. A light application of fertilizer can help boost their growth. Beans fix nitrogen in the soil, making them excellent for crop rotation.

Hot Peppers (Capsicum spp.) Zones 5 to 8 (annuals), Zones 9 to 11 (perennials)

Similar to bell peppers, hot peppers need warm soil and temperatures to thrive. Start seeds indoors 8 to 10 weeks before the last frost and transplant them 14 to 18 inches apart. Seeds generally take 7 to 21 days to germinate. They require full sun and well-drained soil. Keep the soil consistently moist and use mulch to help retain soil moisture. Fertilize with a phosphorus-rich feed to support fruit development. Hot peppers can benefit from companion planting with herbs like basil, which enhances their flavor and helps repel pests.

Kale (Brassica oleracea var. sabellica) Zones 7 to 9

Kale is a hardy vegetable that can be grown in spring and fall. It prefers cool temperatures and can tolerate light frosts. Sow seeds directly in the garden about 4 to 6 weeks before the last frost in spring or 6 to 8 weeks before the first frost in fall. Seeds generally take 5 to 10 days to germinate. Space plants about 12 inches apart in a sunny spot with fertile, well-drained soil. Kale requires consistent moisture and benefits from mulching to retain soil moisture. Fertilize with a balanced vegetable fertilizer to encourage lush, leafy growth.

Lettuce (Lactuca sativa) Zones 4 to 9

Lettuce thrives in cooler climates but can be grown year-round in many areas with some shade and water management. Seeds generally take 7 to 10 days to germinate. It's a quick grower, with seedlings typically ready to transplant in 2 to 3 weeks. Plant them outside about 8 to 12 inches apart in loose, fertile soil. Lettuce needs consistent moisture, especially during dry spells, to maintain its crispness. Fertilization isn't usually necessary if you start with rich soil. A fun fact: Lettuce is a fabulous companion for strawberries, helping to deter some common pests that favor the sweet fruit.

Onions (Allium cepa) Zones 3 to 9

Onions are grown from small bulbs or seedlings and require a long growing season. Seeds generally take 7 to 10 days to germinate. Plant them in early spring, about 4 to 5 inches apart. They prefer full sun and well-drained soil. Onions have shallow roots and require consistent moisture to develop properly. Fertilize with a nitrogen-rich feed in the early stages to promote good leaf growth, which is essential for bulb development.

Parsnips (Pastinaca sativa) Zones 2 to 9

Parsnips are similar to carrots but require a longer growing season. Plant them in early spring, about 2 to 3 weeks before the last frost. They can take up to 3 weeks to germinate and should be thinned to about 3 to 6 inches apart. Parsnips prefer full sun and deep, fertile, well-drained soil. They need consistent moisture to develop well, especially during the growing season. Fertilize with a low-nitrogen, high-potassium fertilizer to encourage root growth.

Peas (Pisum sativum) Zones 2 to 9

Peas are cool-season crops that should be planted early in the spring. Seeds typically take 7 to 14 days to germinate. They take about 4 to 6 weeks from seed to seedlings and can be planted about 2 inches apart. They prefer cooler temperatures and can even tolerate light frosts. Provide support for climbing varieties to encourage vertical growth. Peas need moderate watering, especially once pods begin to form. They are light feeders and generally do not require additional fertilization.

Potatoes (Solanum tuberosum) Zones 3 to 10

Potatoes are cool-season crops that should be planted early in the spring, about 2 weeks before the last frost. They are grown from seed potatoes, pieces of potatoes with eyes, or buds (tubers). Tubers take about 14 to 21 days to sprout after planting. Plant them about 12 inches apart in rows spaced 3 feet apart. Potatoes require deep, loose, well-drained soil to develop properly. Water regularly, especially when plants are flowering and tubers are developing. Avoid over-fertilizing, which can promote more foliage rather than tuber growth.

Radishes (Raphanus sativus) Zones 2 to 10

Radishes are incredibly fast-growing, with some varieties ready to harvest just 3 weeks after planting. They can be grown in both spring and fall, but avoid hot summer months as they will bolt. Sow seeds directly about one inch apart in well-drained soil. Seeds generally take 3 to 10 days to germinate. Radishes need frequent, light watering to keep the soil evenly moist. They require very little fertilization. Radishes are a great catch crop, fitting nicely between slower-growing vegetables like squash.

Rhubarb (Rheum rhabarbarum) Zones 3 to 8

Rhubarb is a perennial vegetable grown for its tart, colorful stalks. Seeds generally take 14 to 21 days to germinate. Rhubarb is commonly propagated by crowns rather than seeds. Plant crowns in early spring, spacing them about 3 feet apart in a sunny, well-drained area. Rhubarb prefers cool temperatures and moist, fertile soil. It requires regular watering, especially during dry periods, and a balanced fertilizer applied in early spring to promote vigorous growth.

Spinach (Spinacia oleracea) Zones 2 to 9

Spinach is a nutrient-rich green that grows best in cool weather. Plant seeds directly in the garden about 4 to 6 weeks before the last frost in spring or 6 to 8 weeks before the first frost in fall. Seeds generally germinate within 7 to 10 days. Space plants about 6 inches apart in fertile, well-drained soil. Spinach needs consistent moisture to prevent bolting. A light application of a balanced fertilizer can enhance growth.

Squash (Cucurbita spp.) Zones 3 to 10

Squash comes in many varieties, including summer and winter versions like zucchini and butternut, respectively. Plant seeds directly in the garden after the last frost when the soil has warmed. Seeds generally take 7 to 10 days to germinate. Space plants about 24 to 36 inches apart in a sunny, well-draining area. Squash requires regular watering, especially during flowering and fruit development. A balanced fertilizer applied at planting and again during the growing season can enhance growth and yield.

Tomatoes (Solanum lycopersicum) Zones 2 to 10

One of the most beloved garden vegetables, tomatoes thrive in warm conditions and should be planted after the last frost. Seeds generally take 5 to 10 days to germinate. They take about 5 to 6 weeks from seed to seedlings and need about 24 to 36 inches of space in sunny spots. Tomatoes require consistent watering to prevent cracking, and a tomato-specific fertilizer can promote vigorous growth and fruitful harvests. They benefit greatly from companion planting with basil or marigolds, which can help repel pests.

Turnips (Brassica rapa subsp. rapa) Zones 2 to 9

Turnips are a fast-growing crop that can be harvested as early as 5 to 8 weeks after planting. They can be grown in spring and fall, as they tolerate light frosts. Sow seeds directly about 2 inches apart and thin to about 4 to 6 inches apart as they grow. Seeds generally take 5 to 10 days to germinate. Turnips prefer full sun and fertile, well-drained soil. Regular watering is necessary for uniform root development. A light application of a balanced fertilizer can be beneficial.

Yardlong Beans (Vigna unguiculata subsp. sesquipedalis) Zones 7 to 10

Yardlong beans, also known as asparagus beans or Chinese long beans, are a warm-season legume that thrives in hot weather and requires a long growing season. Plant seeds directly in the garden 1 to 2 weeks after the last frost when the soil has warmed. Seeds typically germinate in 7 to 14 days. Space plants about 6 inches apart in rows 3 to 4 feet apart, or train them on trellises to save space and improve air circulation. Yardlong beans prefer full sun and well-drained, fertile soil. Consistent moisture is crucial, especially during flowering and pod development. Fertilize with a balanced fertilizer to support healthy growth and pod production.

Zucchini (Cucurbita pepo) Zones 3 to 10

Zucchini is a type of summer squash that grows quickly and produces abundantly. Plant seeds directly in the garden after the last frost when the soil has warmed. Seeds take about 5 to

10 days to germinate. Space plants about 24 inches apart in a sunny, well-draining area. Zucchini requires regular watering, especially during flowering and fruit development. A balanced fertilizer applied at planting and again during the growing season can enhance growth and yield.

The plethora of vegetables is mind-blowing and can offer healthy, delicious, and nutritious variety to your meals. They all start their growth in different ways and prefer all types of different conditions, which can encourage experimentation in your garden or home.

6.2 Herbs

Herbs can sometimes be overlooked in the garden, but they offer a bounty of flavors, fragrances, and even medicinal benefits, all while being delightfully easy to cultivate. Whether you're looking to sprinkle fresh basil on your pizza, sip some soothing mint tea, or savor the aromatic bliss of rosemary and thyme wafting through your garden, growing your own herbs can be incredibly rewarding and surprisingly straightforward.

Basil (Ocimum basilicum) Zones 10 to 11 (perennial), Zones 2 to 9 (after last frost)

Basil is a sun-loving annual herb that thrives in warm weather. Typically, basil seeds will germinate in 5 to 10 days under optimal conditions, with seedlings ready to be transplanted outdoors when they are about 2 to 3 inches tall. Plant basil in a spot that receives sunlight daily, spacing plants about 12 to 18 inches apart. This herb prefers moist, well-drained soil and needs to be watered regularly, especially during dry spells. While basil is not overly demanding regarding fertilizer, a light application of an organic fertilizer can promote lush, flavorful leaves. Basil is wonderful for companion planting with tomatoes, as it can help repel pests like flies and mosquitoes.

Chives (Allium schoenoprasum) Zones 3 to 9

Chives, with their delicate onion flavor, are perennial herbs that are incredibly hardy and easy to grow. They prefer full sun but can tolerate partial shade and are suited to a wide range of climate zones. Chive seeds typically take 10 to 14 days to germinate, and the young seedlings can be planted outside once they reach a height of 2 to 3 inches. Space them about 8 to 12 inches apart in fertile, well-drained soil. Chives require moderate watering and occasional feeding with a balanced organic fertilizer to keep the clumps vigorous. In addition to their culinary uses, chives can deter pests such as Japanese beetles and are excellent planted around rose bushes to enhance growth.

Cilantro (Coriandrum sativum) Zones 2 to 11

Cilantro, or coriander, is a fast-growing annual herb that can be tricky due to its tendency to bolt in hot weather. It's best planted in early spring or fall. Cilantro seeds can take up to 2 to 3 weeks to germinate and should be spaced about 6 to 8 inches apart in light, well-draining soil. This herb prefers cooler conditions and should be placed in an area that receives morning sun and afternoon shade to prevent bolting. Cilantro needs regular watering to keep the soil evenly moist and benefits from occasional feeding with a nitrogen-rich fertilizer. It's a great companion for spinach and beans, helping to deter aphids.

Dill (Anethum graveolens) Zones 2 to 11

Dill is an annual herb that adds a delicate flavor to dishes. It prefers full sun and grows best in well-drained soil. Dill seeds germinate in about 10 to 14 days and should be sown directly in the garden as it doesn't transplant well. Space dill plants about 8 to 12 inches apart. This herb needs regular watering, particularly during dry spells, to develop its feathery fronds and aromatic seeds. Dill is a great companion for cabbage, onions, and cucumbers, attracting beneficial insects that help control pests.

Mint (Mentha spp.) Zones 3 to 11

Mint is a vigorous perennial that can quickly take over the garden if not contained. It thrives in partial shade to full sun and prefers moist, well-drained soil. Mint can be grown from seeds, but starting with root divisions or cuttings is easier. Seeds typically germinate within 10 to 15 days. Plant mint in pots or confined spaces to control its spread. It requires regular watering, especially in hot, dry weather, and benefits from periodic feeding with a balanced fertilizer. Mint's strong scent makes it an excellent companion for cabbage and tomatoes, repelling pests like cabbage moths and aphids.

Parsley (Petroselinum crispum) Zones 7 to 9

Parsley, available in both curly and flat-leaf varieties, is a biennial herb often grown as an annual. It prefers full sun to partial shade and rich, moist soil. Parsley seeds are slow to germinate, typically taking 2 to 3 weeks, and should be spaced about 8 to 10 inches apart. Regular watering and monthly feeding with an organic fertilizer will help maintain vibrant, healthy plants. Parsley is wonderful in any garden, attracting beneficial insects and enhancing the growth and flavor of tomatoes and asparagus when planted nearby.

Rosemary (Rosmarinus officinalis) Zones 7 to 11

Rosemary is a robust, evergreen perennial herb that loves the sun and well-drained soil. It is drought-resistant once established, making it an excellent choice for gardeners in warmer, dry climates. Rosemary can take longer to germinate, sometimes up to a few weeks, and should be spaced about 24 to 36 inches apart to accommodate its woody growth. This herb requires little watering and is best fertilized sparingly to avoid lush leaves at the expense of flavor and aroma. Rosemary's strong scent is wonderful for repelling various pests and is particularly good when planted near beans, cabbage, and carrots.

Sage (Salvia officinalis) Zones 4 to 8

Sage is a perennial herb known for its strong aroma and earthy flavor, making it a staple in many culinary traditions. Sage plants prefer full sun and well-drained slightly sandy soil. They are drought-tolerant once established, requiring only occasional deep watering. Seeds take about 2 to 3 weeks to germinate, and seedlings should be spaced about 18 to 24 inches apart to allow for their bushy growth. Sage is relatively low-maintenance in terms of feeding, needing only a light application of a balanced organic fertilizer in the spring. As a companion plant, sage is beneficial to cabbage and carrots, as it repels common pests like cabbage moths and carrot flies.

Thyme (Thymus vulgaris) Zones 5 to 9

Thyme is a versatile perennial herb that forms a lovely, aromatic ground cover. It prefers full sun but can tolerate light shade and thrives in well-drained soil. Thyme seeds are tiny and can take up to 2 to 3 weeks to germinate. Once the seedlings are sturdy enough, plant them about 12 inches apart. This herb is drought-tolerant and requires minimal watering once established. Thyme benefits from light feeding with an organic fertilizer in the spring. Its sprawling habit makes it an excellent companion for strawberries, as it helps deter worms that may affect the fruit.

Each of these herbs brings its own unique set of flavors, fragrances, and benefits to your garden. By understanding their specific needs and characteristics, you can successfully incorporate them into your gardening endeavors, enhancing both your garden's biodiversity and your culinary repertoire.

6.3 Flowers

Exploring the enchanting world of flowers brings a new dimension of color and fragrance to your garden. Each bloom beautifies your space and supports local ecosystems by attracting pollinators. Let's delve into the specifics of various beloved flowers, ensuring you have all the knowledge to make your garden a vibrant tapestry of blooms.

Azalea (Rhododendron spp.) Zones 4 to 9

Azaleas are popular flowering shrubs known for their vibrant blooms in spring and, in some varieties, again in fall. They are excellent for borders, mass plantings, and as focal points in shaded garden areas. Plant azaleas in early spring or fall to allow them to establish roots before extreme temperatures. Seeds typically germinate within 21 to 60 days, so they are often propagated from cuttings. Space plants about 3 to 5 feet apart, depending on the variety and desired effect. Azaleas prefer partial shade to full shade and well-drained, acidic soil rich in organic matter. Regular watering is important to keep the soil moist but not waterlogged, especially during dry spells. Fertilize with an acidic fertilizer formulated for azaleas and rhododendrons in the spring after flowering to support healthy growth and blooms. Mulching around the plants can help retain soil moisture, maintain soil acidity, and suppress weeds. Pruning immediately after flowering helps maintain shape and encourages more blooms.

Begonia (Begonia spp.) Zones 9 to 11

Begonias are prized for their vibrant flowers and attractive foliage, making them versatile plants for both gardens and containers. They thrive in various conditions and are relatively easy to care for. Begonias thrive in partial shade to full shade. They can tolerate some morning sun but should be protected from intense afternoon sun, which can scorch their leaves. Begonias can be started indoors 8 to 10 weeks before the last frost date and planted in the spring after the danger of frost has passed. Seeds germinate within 14 to 21 days, but begonias are commonly propagated from cuttings or tubers. Plant them about 8 to 12 inches apart. Begonias prefer well-drained, slightly acidic soil rich in organic matter. Water regularly, especially during dry periods. Keep the soil consistently moist but not waterlogged. Amending the soil with compost can improve its fertility and drainage. Use a balanced, water-soluble fertilizer every 2 to 4 weeks during the growing season. Deadheading spent flowers encourages continuous blooming. In colder regions, tuberous begonias can be dug up, stored in a cool, dry place over the winter, and replanted in the spring.

Black-eyed Susan, aka Gloriosa Daisy (Rudbeckia hirta) Zones 3 to 9

Black-eyed Susans are vibrant, summer-blooming, resilient perennials that bring a bright, golden splash to gardens with their bright yellow, orange, or bi-colored petals with dark centers. They are ideal for borders, wildflower gardens, and cutting gardens. They are native to North America, ideal for attracting butterflies and bees, and can tolerate some drought once established. Sow seeds directly in the garden in late spring after the danger of frost has passed, or start them indoors 6 to 8 weeks before the last frost date. Seeds typically germinate anywhere within 7 to 30 days and can be spaced about 12 to 18 inches apart. These flowers prefer full sun and well-drained moderately fertile soil. Regular watering is important to keep the soil consistently moist but not water-logged. They are relatively low-maintenance but appreciate occasional watering during very dry periods and light slow-release fertilization in spring and mid-summer to support healthy growth and abundant blooms. Their daisy-like appearance and durability make them an excellent choice for a beginner gardener looking for reliable summer-long blooms. Deadheading spent flowers encourages continuous blooming throughout the growing season.

Camelia (Camellia spp.) Zones 6 to 9

Camellias are evergreen shrubs known for their beautiful, rose-like flowers that bloom from fall to spring, depending on the species and variety. They are ideal for borders, hedges, and as specimen plants in shaded garden areas. Plant camellias in early spring or fall to allow them to establish roots before extreme temperatures. Seeds typically germinate within 1 to 2 months. Space plants about 5 to 8 feet apart, depending on the variety and desired effect. Camellias prefer partial shade and well-drained, acidic soil rich in organic matter. Regular watering is important to keep the soil moist but not water-logged, especially during dry spells. Fertilize with an acidic fertilizer formulated for camellias and other acid-loving plants in early spring and midsummer to support healthy growth and blooms. Mulching around the plants can help retain soil moisture, maintain soil acidity, and suppress weeds. Pruning after flowering helps maintain shape and encourages more blooms.

Chrysanthemum (Chrysanthemum morifolium) Zones 5 to 9

Chrysanthemums or mums are popular perennials offering a spectacular autumn display. They prefer full sun exposure. Seeds germinate within 10 to 15 days and should be spaced about 18 inches apart. Mums require well-drained soil and benefit from regular watering and fertilization throughout the growing season, especially when buds begin to form. Taller varieties may need staking to support the heavy blooms and prevent the stems from bending or breaking. They are fantastic for borders or containers and are known for their long-lasting blooms, which make excellent cut flowers. Additionally, chrysanthemums are celebrated for their ability to repel common garden pests such as beetles.

Daffodil (Narcissus spp.) Zones 3 to 9

Daffodils are popular spring-blooming perennials known for their bright, trumpet-shaped flowers in shades of yellow, white, and orange. They are ideal for borders, rock gardens, and naturalized areas. Seeds can take several years to germinate and are commonly propagated from bulbs. Plant daffodil bulbs in the fall, about 2 to 4 weeks before the ground freezes, allowing them to establish roots before winter. Space bulbs about 3 to 6 inches apart and plant them 6 inches deep, with the pointed end up. Daffodils prefer full sun to partial shade and well-drained soil rich in organic matter. They require regular watering after planting and during their growing season but prefer dry conditions during dormancy. Fertilize with a balanced bulb fertilizer at planting time and again in early spring as growth begins. Deadhead spent flowers but allow the foliage to die back naturally to replenish the bulb for the next season.

Dahlia (Dahlia spp.) Zones 8 to 11

Dahlias are vibrant, summer-blooming perennials known for their large, showy flowers that come in various colors and shapes. They are ideal for borders and container gardening. Seeds typically germinate within 7 to 14 days; however, dahlias are commonly propagated from tubers. Plant dahlia tubers in the spring after the danger of frost has passed and the soil has warmed. Space tubers about 18 to 24 inches apart, depending on the variety, and plant them about 6 inches deep. Dahlias prefer full sun and well-drained, fertile soil rich in organic matter. Regular watering is essential to keep the soil consistently moist but not waterlogged, especially during dry spells. Fertilize with a balanced, water-soluble fertilizer every 2 to 4 weeks during the growing season to support vigorous growth and abundant blooms. Staking taller varieties helps support the heavy flower heads. Deadheading spent flowers encourages continuous blooming throughout the growing season. Tubers can be dug up and stored indoors for the winter.

Daylily (Hemerocallis spp.) Zones 3 to 9

Daylilies are hardy perennials known for their vibrant, trumpet-shaped flowers that bloom profusely throughout the summer. These plants are excellent for borders, ground covers, and mass plantings. Plant daylilies in early spring or early fall, giving them time to establish before extreme temperatures. Seeds typically germinate within 4 to 6 weeks. Space plants about 18 to 24 inches apart to allow for proper growth and airflow. Daylilies prefer full sun to partial shade and well-drained, fertile soil. They are relatively drought-tolerant once established but benefit from regular watering, especially during dry spells. Fertilize with a balanced fertilizer in the spring and midsummer to support vigorous growth and blooming. Deadheading can encourage continued blooming and maintain plant health.

Foxglove (Digitalis purpurea) Zones 4 to 10

Foxgloves are biennials or short-lived perennials known for their tall spikes of bell-shaped flowers. They prefer partial shade, although they can tolerate full sun in cooler climates. Foxglove seeds can take 14 to 21 days to germinate and should be planted about 12 to 18 inches apart in moist, well-drained soil. They require regular watering, particularly in dry weather, and benefit from a general-purpose fertilizer applied in early spring. Foxgloves are particularly loved for their vertical interest in garden designs and their ability to attract hummingbirds. However, it's important to note that **all parts of the foxglove plant are toxic if ingested**, so they should be planted with caution in gardens frequented by pets and children.

Geranium (Pelargonium spp.) Zones 2 to 9 (annuals), Zones 10 to 11 (perennials)

Geraniums are popular garden plants known for their vibrant blooms and attractive foliage. They are versatile and can be used in borders, containers, hanging baskets, and as ground covers. Plant geraniums in the spring after the last frost. They can also be started indoors 6 to 8 weeks before the last frost. Seeds germinate typically within 7 to 14 days. Space plants about 8 to 12 inches apart, depending on the variety and desired effect. Geraniums prefer well-drained soil that is moderately fertile with a slightly acidic to neutral pH. Water geraniums when the soil feels dry to the touch. Avoid overwatering, as geraniums are prone to root rot in soggy soil. Fertilize every 4 to 6 weeks during the growing season with a balanced, water-soluble fertilizer to promote healthy growth and blooming. Deadhead spent flowers regularly to encourage continuous blooming. In perennial zones, cut back the plants in the fall to encourage new growth in the spring.

Hosta (Hosta spp.) Zones 3 to 9

Hostas are popular shade-tolerant perennials known for their attractive foliage and low maintenance requirements. These plants are ideal for borders, ground covers, and shaded garden areas. Plant hostas in early spring or fall, allowing them to establish roots before extreme temperatures. Seeds typically germinate within 14 to 21 days; however, hostas are commonly propagated by division. Space plants about 18 to 36 inches apart, depending on the variety, to allow for their mature size. Hostas prefer partial to full shade and well-drained, fertile soil rich in organic matter. They require regular watering, especially during dry spells, to keep the soil consistently moist but not waterlogged. Fertilize with a balanced fertilizer in the spring and midsummer to support healthy growth and vibrant foliage. Mulching around the plants can help retain soil moisture and suppress weeds. Hostas are relatively low maintenance but may require protection from slugs and snails, which are common pests.

Hydrangea (Hydrangea spp.) Zones 3 to 9

Hydrangeas are popular ornamental shrubs known for their large, showy flower clusters that can change color based on soil pH. They are excellent for borders, hedges, and as focal points in garden beds. Plant hydrangeas in early spring or fall to allow them to establish before extreme temperatures. Seeds germinate within 14 to 28 days, but hydrangea is commonly propagated by cuttings or divisions. Space plants about 3 to 10 feet apart, depending on the variety and desired effect. Hydrangeas prefer partial shade to full sun and well-drained, fertile soil rich in organic matter. Regular watering is important to keep the soil moist but not waterlogged, especially during dry spells. Fertilize with a balanced fertilizer in spring and midsummer to support healthy growth and abundant blooms. Mulching around the plants can help retain soil moisture and suppress weeds. Pruning is necessary to maintain shape and encourages vigorous flowering, and the timing and method vary depending on the species.

Iris (Iris spp.) Zones 3 to 9

Irises are popular perennials known for their striking, sword-like foliage and beautiful, intricate flowers in various colors. They are excellent for borders, rock gardens, and as focal points in garden beds. Irises thrive in full sun but can tolerate partial shade. Seeds typically germinate within 30 to 90 days; however, irises are commonly propagated from rhizomes or bulbs. Plant their rhizomes about 12 to 24 inches apart in the early spring or late summer to early fall. Irises prefer well-drained soil rich in organic matter and do best in slightly acidic to neutral pH. Water regularly during the growing season to keep the soil moist but not waterlogged. Reduce watering after plants have finished blooming to prevent rot. Amend the soil with compost or well-rotted manure to improve fertility and drainage. Fertilize in early spring with a balanced fertilizer with a second application after flowering to build rhizomes for the next season. Deadheading spent flowers encourages continuous blooming throughout the growing season.

Lavender (Lavandula spp.) Zones 5 to 9

Lavender is a popular perennial herb known for its fragrant flowers and foliage, making it a staple in herb gardens and landscapes. Lavender thrives in warm, sunny conditions and should be planted in the spring after the danger of frost has passed. Seeds typically take about 14 to 28 days to germinate, but starting with young plants or cuttings can be more reliable. Plant seeds or transplants 12 to 18 inches apart for proper air circulation and growth. Lavender prefers full sun and well-drained slightly alkaline soil. It is drought-tolerant once established but benefits from regular watering during its first year. Fertilization is generally not necessary; however, a light application of a balanced fertilizer can be applied in the spring if the soil is poor. Lavender is excellent for attracting pollinators and can be used in cooking, crafts, and aromatherapy.

Lily (Lilium spp.) Zones 3 to 9

Lilies are elegant perennials known for their large, showy flowers and sweet fragrance, making them popular choices for gardens and floral arrangements. These plants are ideal for borders, beds, and containers. Seeds germinate within 30 to 180 days, but lilies are more commonly propagated from bulbs. Plant lily bulbs in the fall or early spring, about 6 to 8 inches deep, and space them 8 to 12 inches apart. Lilies prefer full sun to partial shade and well-drained, fertile soil rich in organic matter. They require regular watering, especially during the growing season, to keep the soil consistently moist but not waterlogged. Fertilize with a balanced fertilizer in the spring and midsummer to promote healthy growth and blooming. Deadheading spent flowers can encourage continued blooming, and mulching can help retain soil moisture and keep roots cool.

Lily-of-the-Valley (Convallaria majalis) Zones 3 to 8

Lily-of-the-Valley is a fragrant, shade-loving perennial known for its dainty, bell-shaped white flowers that bloom in late spring. It is ideal for ground covers, shaded garden areas, and woodland gardens. Seeds are slow to germinate, often taking several months, so lily-of-the-valley is commonly propagated from rhizomes. Plant Lily-of-the-Valley rhizomes (often called "pips") in early spring or fall to allow them to establish roots before extreme temperatures. Space rhizomes about 1 to 2 feet apart, allowing them room to spread. Lily-of-the-Valley prefers partial to full shade and well-drained, humus-rich soil. Regular watering is important to keep the soil consistently moist, especially during dry spells. Fertilization is generally unnecessary, but a light application of a balanced fertilizer in early spring can support growth. After blooming, the foliage remains attractive and helps to maintain the plant's health. It is important to note that **all parts of the lily-of-the-valley are highly toxic if ingested**.

Marigold (Tagetes spp.) Zones 1 to 13 (annuals)

Marigolds are popular for their bright, cheerful flowers and ability to repel pests, making them a great addition to any garden. These annuals thrive in warm temperatures and should be planted outside after the danger of frost has passed. They typically take about 5 to 7 days to germinate from seed. Plant seeds about 1/4 inch deep and 6 to 12 inches apart, depending on the variety. Marigolds prefer full sun and well-drained soil. They are drought-tolerant but benefit from regular watering, especially during dry spells. Fertilize with a balanced fertilizer to encourage prolific blooming. Marigolds are excellent companions for vegetables like tomatoes and peppers, helping to deter pests naturally.

Nasturtium (Tropaeolum majus) Zones 1 to 13 (annuals)

Nasturtiums are valued for their vibrant, edible flowers and peppery leaves, making them a colorful and functional addition to any garden. These annuals thrive in warm temperatures and can be planted outside after the danger of frost has passed. They typically take about 7 to 10 days to germinate from seed. Plant seeds about 1/2 inch deep and space plants 8 to 12 inches apart for proper growth and airflow. Nasturtiums prefer full sun to partial shade and well-drained, moderately fertile soil. They are relatively drought-tolerant but benefit from regular watering, especially during dry spells. Avoid excessive fertilization, as this can lead to lush foliage at the expense of flowers. Nasturtiums are excellent companions for vegetables like cucumbers and tomatoes, helping to repel pests naturally.

Pansy (Viola tricolor var. hortensis) Zones 6 to 10

Pansies are beloved for their colorful, cheerful flowers that can bloom in cool weather, making them an excellent choice for spring and fall gardens. These annuals thrive in cooler temperatures and should be planted outside in early spring or late summer. They typically take about 7 to 15 days to germinate from seed. Plant seeds about 1/8 inch deep and space plants 6 to 8 inches apart for proper growth and airflow. Pansies prefer full sun to partial shade and well-drained, fertile soil rich in organic matter. Regular watering is essential, especially during dry spells, as pansies prefer consistently moist soil. Fertilize with a balanced fertilizer to encourage continuous blooming. Pansies are excellent for adding color to garden borders, containers, and hanging baskets.

Peony (Paeonia spp.) Zones 3 to 8

Peonies are beloved perennials known for their large, fragrant blooms and long lifespan, making them a staple in gardens and floral arrangements. These plants are ideal for borders, beds, and as focal points in the garden. Seeds typically germinate within 5 months to 2 years, and peonies are commonly propagated from root divisions. Plant peony tubers in the fall, about 2 to 3 inches deep, ensuring the eyes (buds) are facing upward, and space them 3 to 4 feet apart to allow for their mature size. Peonies prefer full sun to partial shade and well-drained, fertile soil rich in organic matter. They require regular watering, especially during dry spells, to keep the soil consistently moist but not waterlogged. Fertilize with a balanced fertilizer in early spring and again after blooming to promote healthy growth and flowering. Peonies benefit from being mulched to retain soil moisture and protect roots from temperature extremes.

Petunia (Petunia spp.) Zones 1 to 13 (annual)

Petunias are popular annuals known for their vibrant, trumpet-shaped flowers that bloom profusely throughout the growing season. They are excellent for borders, hanging baskets, containers, and as ground covers. Sow petunia seeds indoors 10-12 weeks before the last frost date or purchase young plants from a nursery. Germination typically takes 7 to 10 days. Space plants about 6 to 12 inches apart, depending on the variety, to allow for proper growth and airflow. Petunias prefer full sun and well-drained soil. Regular watering is important to keep the soil consistently moist but not water-logged. Fertilize with a balanced, water-soluble fertilizer every 2 to 3 weeks during the growing season to support healthy growth and abundant blooms. Deadheading spent flowers encourages continuous blooming throughout the growing season. Petunias make excellent companion plants for vegetables and other flowers, helping to attract pollinators and beneficial insects.

Roses (Rosa spp.) Zones 3 to 10

Roses are renowned for their beautiful, fragrant blooms and come in various colors and varieties. They are ideal for borders, hedges, containers, and as focal points in the garden. Plant roses in early spring or fall to allow them to establish roots before extreme temperatures. Seeds typically germinate within 6 to 12 weeks, but roses are commonly propagated from cuttings, grafting, or bare root plants. Space plants about 2 to 3 feet apart, depending on the variety and growth habit. Roses prefer full sun and well-drained, fertile soil rich in organic matter. Regular watering is important to keep the soil consistently moist but not waterlogged, especially during dry spells. Fertilize with a balanced, slow-release fertilizer in early spring and again in mid-summer to support healthy growth and abundant blooms. Pruning in late winter or early spring helps maintain shape, remove dead or diseased wood, and encourages more flowers.

Sunflower (Helianthus annuus) Zones 1 to 13 (annual)

Sunflowers are loved for their tall stature and vibrant, sunny blooms, perfect for a sunny spot in your garden. These annuals thrive in warm temperatures and should be planted outside after the danger of frost has passed. They typically take about 7 to 10 days to germinate from seed. Plant seeds about 1 inch deep and 6 inches apart, thinning to 12-18 inches apart once they are a few inches tall. Sunflowers prefer full sun and well-drained soil enriched with compost or organic matter. They are relatively drought-tolerant but benefit from regular watering, especially during dry spells. A balanced fertilizer can encourage strong growth and larger blooms. Sunflowers are also great companions for cucumbers, squash, and corn, helping to attract pollinators and provide natural support for climbing plants.

Sweet Pea (Lathyrus odoratus) Zones 1 to 13 (annual)

Sweet peas are cherished for their fragrant and colorful flowers, perfect for a sunny or partially shaded garden spot. These annuals thrive in cooler temperatures and should be planted outside after the danger of frost has passed. They typically take about 10 to 21 days to germinate from seed. Plant them about 5 inches apart, and they'll need a trellis or some support to climb. Sweet peas like moist, well-drained soil and benefit from regular watering, especially during dry spells. A light application of a low-nitrogen fertilizer can encourage more blooms. Known for their cut flower quality, sweet peas are also great companions for beans and carrots, helping to deter pests naturally.

Tulip (Tulipa spp.) Zones 3 to 8

Tulips are popular spring-blooming perennials known for their vibrant, cup-shaped flowers that come in a wide range of colors. They are ideal for borders, containers, and mass plantings in garden beds. Plant tulip bulbs in the fall, about 6 to 8 weeks before the ground freezes, allowing them to establish roots before winter. Seeds can take several years to germinate, and tulips are commonly propagated from bulbs. Space bulbs about 4 to 6 inches apart and plant them 6 to 8 inches deep, with the pointed end up. Tulips prefer full sun to partial shade and well-drained soil rich in organic matter. They require regular watering after planting and during their growing season but prefer dry conditions during dormancy. Fertilize with a balanced bulb fertilizer at planting time and again in early spring as growth begins. Deadhead spent flowers but allow the foliage to die back naturally to replenish the bulb for the next season. In warmer zones, tulips are annuals, and bulbs should be pre-chilled in a paper bag in the refrigerator, away from fruits and vegetables that release ethylene gas. Pre-chill for 12 to 16 weeks before planting.

Zinnia (Zinnia spp.) Zones 1 to 13 (annuals)

Zinnias are known for their bright, cheerful blooms that come in various colors and shapes. They are excellent for borders, cutting gardens, and containers. Sow zinnia seeds directly in the garden after the danger of frost has passed, or start them indoors 4-6 weeks before the last frost date. Germination typically takes 7 to 10 days. Space plants about 6 to 18 inches apart, depending on the variety, to allow for proper growth and airflow. Zinnias prefer full sun and well-drained soil. Regular watering is important to keep the soil consistently moist but not waterlogged. Fertilize with a balanced, water-soluble fertilizer every 4 to 6 weeks during the growing season to support healthy growth and abundant blooms. Dead-heading spent flowers encourages continuous blooming throughout the growing season.

These flowers, each with their unique requirements and charms, offer endless possibilities for enhancing your garden's aesthetic and ecological diversity. By understanding the specific needs of each flower, from soil preferences to spacing and watering requirements, you can create a beautiful and flourishing garden.

6.4 Fruit

Imagine walking through your garden, under the shade of fruit-laden branches, plucking a sun-warmed berry or slicing open a freshly picked melon. Growing your own fruit can be a delightful and rewarding aspect of gardening, offering fresh flavors in the harvest right from your backyard. Let's explore the care and cultivation of various popular fruits, ensuring you can enjoy these sweet rewards season after season.

Apples (Malus domestica) Zones 4 to 8

Apple trees are deciduous and are known for their sweet, crisp fruits and can be grown in various climates. Plant apple trees in early spring or fall to allow them to establish before extreme temperatures. Seeds germinate within 1 to 6 weeks;

however, apple trees are commonly propagated from grafting onto rootstocks. Space plants about 15 to 20 feet apart, depending on the variety and rootstock. Apples prefer full sun and well-drained, fertile soil with a pH of 6.0 to 7.0. Regular watering is important to keep the soil consistently moist but not waterlogged, especially during dry spells. Fertilize with a balanced fertilizer in early spring and again in mid-summer to support healthy growth and fruit production. Pruning helps maintain shape, removes dead or diseased wood, and encourages better air circulation and fruiting. Mulching helps retain soil moisture and suppress weeds. Most varieties require cross-pollination from another apple variety to produce fruit. Pick apples when their skin color has changed from green to the color typical of the variety. Gently lift or twist the apple, and if it's ready to be picked, it should come easily off the branch with its stem attached.

Blackberries (Rubus fruticosus) Zones 5 to 10

Similar to raspberries, blackberries are hardy and prolific. They require about 3 to 4 weeks from seed to seedling. Seeds can be slow to germinate, often taking several months; therefore, blackberries are commonly propagated from root cuttings or suckers. Plant them in early spring, spacing them 24 to 36 inches apart in rows 6 to 8 feet apart. Blackberries thrive in full sun and well-drained soil, needing consistent watering during the growing season, especially when fruits are developing. Fertilize with a balanced fertilizer in early spring to promote growth and fruit production. Blackberries benefit from trellising to support their growth and make harvesting easier. Harvest blackberries when their color changes from red or purple to a deep, rich black. Ripe berries should be full and plump, yield to gentle pressure, and come off the plant easily when gently pulled.

Blueberries (Vaccinium spp.) Zones 3 to 10

Blueberries, known for their antioxidant properties, prefer acidic soil. They can take several weeks to germinate and should be spaced about 4 to 5 feet apart to allow for mature growth. Blueberries require a soil pH between 4.5 and 5.5; amend your soil with sulfur. They need consistent moisture, especially as the fruit sets. Fertilize with an acid-forming fertilizer to maintain the pH level and support growth. Planting blueberries near hydrangeas can help you monitor the soil's acidity, as both require similar conditions. Most blueberry varieties are self-pollinating but produce larger and more abundant fruit when cross-pollinated with another variety. Harvest blueberries when their color uniformly becomes a deep blue or almost black with no hints of red or green. The berries should come off the plant easily with a gentle tug.

Cantaloupe (Cucumis melo) Zones 1 to 13 (annual)

Cantaloupes, or muskmelons, offer sweet, fragrant flesh. These melons require about 5 to 10 days for seeds to germinate and should be planted outdoors after the last frost when the soil warms up. Space them about 36 inches apart in a sunny, well-drained spot in your garden. Cantaloupes need consistent moisture, especially during the peak of summer, to prevent the fruit from drying out. A balanced fertilizer applied every four to six weeks during the growing season supports their vigorous growth and fruit production. Cantaloupes benefit from companion planting with flowers like marigolds, which can help repel pests. They require pollination and can be hand-pollinated if pollination is poor. When it is ripe, the fruit will separate from the vine with a gentle tug (skin golden color and fruit with sweet fragrance).

Figs (Ficus carica) Zones 6 to 11

Figs are a luxurious addition to any garden. Seeds typically germinate within 8 to 12 weeks; however, figs are commonly propagated from cuttings. Plant in early spring and space fig trees about 10 to 20 feet apart, depending on the variety. They prefer well-drained soil and a protected location with full sun. Figs need moderate watering, especially in dry conditions, but do not like overly wet soil. Use a low-nitrogen, high-phosphorus fertilizer to promote fruit development without excessive leaf growth. Figs are self-fertile, so you don't need multiple plants for pollination. The fruit should be slightly soft to the touch and may bend at the neck when ready to harvest. Figs do not ripen off the tree, so pick them when they are fully ripe.

Grapes (Vitis spp.) Zones 4 to 10

Grapevines are deciduous, woody vines known for their sweet and juicy fruits, enjoyed fresh, dried (as raisins), or used for making wine. They are ideal for home gardens. Plant grapevines in early spring to allow them to establish before the growing season. Seeds typically germinate within 2 to 8 weeks; however, grapes are commonly propagated from cuttings. Space plants about 6 to 10 feet apart, depending on the variety and training system. Grapes prefer full sun and well-drained, fertile soil with a pH of 5.5 to 7.0. Regular watering is important to keep the soil consistently moist but not waterlogged, especially during dry spells. Fertilize with a balanced fertilizer in early spring and again in mid-summer to support healthy growth and fruit production. Pruning is essential for maintaining shape, removing dead or diseased wood, and encouraging better air circulation and fruiting. Training the vines on a trellis or arbor helps support the weight of the fruit and ensures better sunlight exposure. Mulching helps retain soil moisture and suppress weeds. Grapes are typically self-pollinating and should be picked when they are fully ripe, as they do not continue to ripen once picked.

Lemons (Citrus limon) Zones 9 to 11

Like most citrus, Lemons are usually grown from seedlings rather than seeds. Seeds germinate within 2 to 6 weeks, but lemons are often propagated from grafting or cuttings. Plant them in a sunny, wind-protected area about 12 to 25 feet apart, depending on the variety. Lemons require well-drained soil and regular watering, but be careful not to over-water. They benefit greatly from citrus-specific fertilizers, which help develop strong branches and vibrant fruits. Lemon trees are typically self-pollinating but can produce more fruit when cross-pollinated with another citrus variety. Harvest when the fruit has a slight give when gently squeezed. Lemons do not continue to ripen off the tree, so it's essential to harvest them when they are mature.

Limes (Citrus aurantiifolia) Zones 9 to 11

Limes are similar in cultural needs to lemons. Plant seedlings rather than seeds, spacing them about 10 to 20 feet apart, depending on the variety. Limes prefer full sun and well-drained soil. Regular, deep watering is important, but ensure good drainage to prevent root rot. Fertilize with a citrus-specific fertilizer to support healthy growth and fruit production. Like lemons, limes can also be grown in containers, making them suitable for smaller spaces or cooler climates where they can be moved indoors during winter. Lime trees are typically self-pollinating but can produce more fruit when cross-pollinated with another citrus variety. Harvest when the fruit has a slight give when gently squeezed. Limes do not continue to ripen off the tree, so it's essential to harvest them when they are mature.

Peach (Prunus persica) Zones 5 to 9

Peach trees are deciduous and prized for their sweet, juicy fruits. Seeds typically require a cold stratification period of about 12 weeks and germinate within 4 to 6 weeks after stratification. Peaches are commonly propagated from grafted rootstock. Plant peach trees in early spring or fall to give them time to establish before extreme temperatures. Space plants about 15 to 20 feet apart, depending on the variety and rootstock. Peaches prefer full sun and well-drained, fertile soil. Regular watering is crucial to keep the soil consistently moist but not waterlogged, especially during dry spells. Fertilize with a balanced fertilizer in early spring and again in mid-summer to support healthy growth and fruit production. Pruning is essential to maintain the tree's shape, remove dead or diseased wood, and encourages better air circulation and fruiting. Mulching helps retain soil moisture and suppress weeds. Most peach tree varieties are self-pollinating. Harvest peaches when they are fully colored and slightly soft to the touch. The fruit should come off the tree easily when gently twisted. Peaches do not ripen significantly off the tree, so harvest when mature.

Pear (Pyrus spp.) Zones 4 to 9 depending upon variety

Pear trees are deciduous and known for their sweet, juicy fruits. Seeds require a cold stratification of about 60 to 90 days and germinate within 2 to 3 weeks after stratification. Pears are commonly propagated from grafted rootstock. Plant pear trees in early spring or fall to allow them to establish before extreme temperatures. Space plants about 15 to 20 feet apart, depending on the variety and rootstock. Pears prefer full sun and well-drained, fertile soil with a pH of 6.0 to 7.0. Regular watering is important to keep the soil consistently moist but not waterlogged, especially during dry spells. Fertilize with a balanced fertilizer in early spring and again in mid-summer to support healthy growth and fruit production. Pruning helps maintain shape, remove dead or diseased wood, and encourages better air circulation and fruiting. Mulching helps retain soil moisture and suppress weeds. Most varieties require cross-pollination, although some are self-pollinating but still benefit from cross-pollination. Harvest pears when mature but still firm and when the fruit comes off easily with a gentle twist.

Plum (Prunus domestica) Zones 4 to 9

Plum trees are deciduous and known for their sweet, juicy fruits that come in various colors, including purple, red, and yellow. They are ideal for temperate climates. Seeds typically require a cold stratification period of about 60 to 90 days and germinate within 4 to 6 weeks; however, plums are commonly propagated from grafted rootstock. Plant plum trees in early spring or fall to allow them to establish before extreme temperatures. Space plants about 15 to 20 feet apart, depending on the variety and rootstock. Plums prefer full sun and well-drained, fertile soil with a pH of 6.0 to 7.5. Regular watering is important to keep the soil consistently moist but not waterlogged, especially during dry spells. Fertilize with a balanced fertilizer in early spring and again in mid-summer to support healthy growth and fruit production. Pruning helps maintain shape, remove dead or diseased wood, and encourages better air circulation and fruiting. Mulching helps retain soil moisture and suppress weeds. Most varieties require cross-pollination, and some are self-pollinating but benefit from cross-pollination. Harvest when they are fully colored and slightly soft to the touch. Fruit should come off the tree easily when gently twisted and should be harvested when they are mature.

Raspberries (Rubus idaeus) Zones 3 to 9

Raspberries are vigorous growers and benefit from support structures such as trellises or stakes to keep them upright and off the ground. Seeds typically germinate within 2 to 4 weeks; however, raspberries are commonly propagated from root cuttings or suckers. They need about 3 to 4 weeks from seed to seedling and prefer a sunny location with well-drained soil. Space raspberry canes about 24 inches apart, with rows spaced about 6 feet apart to accommodate their growth. Regular pruning is essential to maintain their productivity. Raspberries require even moisture and benefit from a mulch layer to retain soil moisture and suppress weeds. An all-purpose fertilizer applied in early spring encourages healthy new growth. They are self-pollinating but benefit from the presence of pollinators to improve fruit and yield. Harvest when they are fully colored and easily come off the plant with a gentle pull. Raspberries do not continue to ripen after being picked, so harvest them when they are mature.

Strawberries (Fragaria × ananassa) Zones 3 to 10

Strawberries are a beloved choice for gardeners of all levels due to their ease of growth and sweet reward. Seeds typically germinate within 2 to 4 weeks; however, strawberries are commonly propagated from runners. Strawberries should be planted in early spring or late fall. From seed to seedling takes approximately 2 to 3 weeks. Space them about 18 to 24 inches apart in rich, fertile soil with full sun exposure. Strawberries require regular watering to keep the soil moist but not soggy. Use a high-potassium fertilizer to encourage vibrant, sweet fruits. Strawberries are excellent when planted near borage, which improves their growth and flavor while deterring pests. Strawberries are self-pollinating but benefit from the presence of pollinators to enhance fruit and yield. Harvest when fully colored and firm, typically in the morning when they are cool. Pull berries from the plant, leaving the green cap attached to the remaining stem. Strawberries do not ripen after being picked, so harvest when mature.

Watermelon (Citrullus lanatus) Zones 1 to 13 (annual)

Watermelons are the quintessence of summer, offering juicy refreshment and thriving in warmer climates. Seeds typically germinate within 4 to 10 days. From seed to seedling, expect about 3 to 4 weeks, planting them outdoors when temperatures consistently exceed 70°F. Space plants about 36 to 60 inches apart to accommodate their sprawling vines. Watermelons require ample watering to develop their characteristic large, juicy fruits, particularly during the fruit setting and growing stages. Fertilize with a phosphorus-rich formula early in the season to promote healthy root development, followed by a nitrogen-focused feed as vines develop. Interestingly, watermelons have a mutually beneficial relationship with radishes that can help deter pests naturally. Watermelons require pollination to fruit, so if pollination is poor, they can be hand-pollinated. Harvest when the fruit is fully mature and look for signs such as a dull skin surface, a yellow spot on the underside where the fruit rested on the ground, and a hollow sound when tapped. The tendril closest to the fruit should be dry and brown. Cut the fruit from the vine with a sharp knife or pruning shears to avoid damage to the rest of the vine.

Growing fruit in your garden adds a layer of enjoyment, providing fresh, delicious produce right at your fingertips. Each fruit type brings its own set of requirements and rewards, enriching your gardening experience and broadening your horticultural skills.

Conclusion

As we draw the curtains on this journey through the enchanting world of raised bed and container gardening, it's time to pause and reflect on the ground we've covered together. From those first decisions about where to place your garden and what materials to use, to understanding the intricacies of soil health and choosing the right plants for your space, you've embarked on a transformative path. Whether you began as a complete novice or someone looking to revise their green thumb, this book has walked you through each step towards becoming a confident gardener.

We've navigated the basics together, learning to appreciate the rhythm of nature and the joy of watching a seed grow into a flourishing plant. The key to a rewarding garden lies in starting small and embracing each learning opportunity. Gardening is not just about the harvest—it's about the daily wonders and the surprises, the trials, and the triumphs.

Every plant that thrives and every challenge overcome is a celebration of your dedication. Gardening, with its inevitable ups and downs, teaches us resilience and offers unparalleled opportunities for personal growth. It's about finding peace in the process, even on the days when the pests seem relentless or the weather uncooperative.

Beyond the boundaries of your garden, remember that with each plant you nurture, you're contributing to a healthier planet. Gardening is a powerful act of sustainability, enhancing biodiversity and fostering a more sustainable relationship with our environment.

As you continue on your gardening adventure, I encourage you to keep exploring, experimenting, and expanding your knowledge. Join local gardening clubs or online communities; these connections can be invaluable sources of support and inspiration. Share your triumphs and challenges, and let the collective wisdom of fellow gardeners guide you.

I invite you to create a garden that truly reflects who you are —your values, interests, and aesthetics. Let your garden be a canvas for your creativity and a space that brings you happiness and peace.

In closing, I want to express my heartfelt belief in your ability to cultivate a thriving garden. No matter your starting point or the size of your space, you have the power to bring a little more green into the world. I am confident that you have the skills necessary to expand and grow your garden year after year. May your gardening journey be filled with curiosity, satisfaction, and a deepening connection with the natural world.

I would love to hear about your gardening experiences, your successes, and the lessons learned along the way. Please feel free to share your stories and feedback with me, as your insights are incredibly valuable. You can email me at: cynggbarre@gmail.com. Happy gardening!

Share Your Thoughts and Make a Difference!

Dear Friends,

We've come to the end of our journey...only to realize that there is a whole host of possibilities for continued learning and now teaching others with your new skills. I am certain that there are other "would-be" gardeners out there who would benefit from learning the basics. Won't you help me convince them that raised bed and container gardening is an endeavor worthy of undertaking?

Please take just a moment to provide an honest and constructive on-line review if you haven't already done so. Any and all support is greatly appreciated! Scan the QR code below, and you'll be taken directly to the review page.

Thank you again for staying the course and reaping the benefits of your toil. My hope is that you'll continue your new gardening lifestyle and find pleasure in connecting with the earth. 'Bye for now!

GG Barre

Helpful Terms and Definitions

These terms will help you in your navigation of this book and interpretation of seed packets, among other things.

Term	Definition
Acidic	Soil or medium that has a pH level below 7.0. The pH scale ranges from 0 to 14, with 7.0 being neutral.
Alkaline	Soil or medium that has a pH level above 7.0.
Annual	A plant that does not survive beyond one growing season and that must be replanted each year. Examples are tomatoes, beans, and petunias.
Biennial	A plant that completes its life cycle over two growing seasons. They produce leaves, stems, and roots in the first year, typically go dormant during the winter, and then flower and produce seeds in the second year.
Bolting	Premature production of a flowering stem before the plant is ready for harvest. This can occur when the plant is stressed by heat or drought.
Cane	Long, slender, and often woody stems of certain plants. Examples are raspberries, grapes, and roses.
Chlorophyll	Green pigment found in plants, algae, and cyanobacteria which plays a crucial role in photosynthesis. Reflects green light which is why plants appear green.
Clay	Inorganic component of soil with the smallest particle size. Small spaces between particles leading to poor drainage and aeration
Corm	Underground storage organ used by certain plants to survive adverse conditions and to reproduce. Not to be confused with bulbs which are composed of layered scales or modified leaves. Examples of corms are crocus and taro.
Crown	Located at the base of the plant where the stem transitions into the root system. New shoots and roots emerge from this part of the plant.
Deadhead	Practice of removing spent or faded flowers from plants just above the first set of healthy leaves or flower buds by cutting with shears or pinching with fingers. Deadheading encourages production of more flowers, prevents self-seeding, and promotes plant health.
Deciduous	Trees that shed their leaves annually, typically in the fall.

Evergreen	Trees that retain their leaves throughout the year.
Grafting	Technique used to join parts from two plants so that they grow as a single plant. Can be used to combine the best characteristics of two plants and grow plants difficult to propagate by seeds or cuttings. Typically a branch is joined to a rootstock.
Humus	The organic material in soil that results from the decomposition of organic matter by microorganisms and is typically dark brown or black with a crumbly texture. Humus is rich in nutrients such as nitrogen, phosphorus, and potassium.
Loam	An ideal mixture of sand, silt, and clay in a ratio of approximately 40% sand, 40% silt, and 20% clay.
Naturalized areas	Sections of a garden or landscape designed and maintained to resemble a natural ecosystem. They are typically characterized with a mix of native and non-native species that can coexist with the local environment and requires minimal maintenance. Examples include wildflower meadows and prairies.
Offset	Young plant that develops from the base or side of a mature parent plant and can be used to propagate new plants (aka pups). Examples include succulents, bulbs such as from tulips and daffodils, and spider plants.
Perennial	A plant that survives for at least several years. Perennials will go into dormancy typically during the winter when conditions are unfavorable and then sprout new growth when conditions are favorable. Examples are strawberries, hostas, and sage.
Photosynthesis	Process by which plants convert light energy (sunlight) into chemical energy stored in the form of glucose (a type of sugar). Fundamental for plant growth and health. Carbon dioxide is taken in and oxygen is produced.
Rhizome	Underground plant stem that grows horizontally beneath the soil surface to produce roots and shoots at intervals along their length. Examples are iris, ginger, and mint.
Rootstock	Root system and sometimes a portion of the lower stem that provides the foundation for a grafted plant.

Runners	Long, horizontal stems that grow from the base on a parent plant and can be used for propagation. Examples include strawberries and mint.
Sand	Inorganic component of soil with the largest particle size. Large spaces between particles which allows for good drainage and aeration but poor water and nutrient retention.
Silt	Inorganic component of soil with medium particle size, moderate drainage and nutrient retention properties.
Slips	Young plant shoot or sprout that is used for propagation and associated with certain types of plants such as potatoes and pineapples.
Spathe	Modified leaf that encloses a flower cluster and plays a key role in attracting pollinators or protecting the flowers they enclose. Examples are calla lilies and anthuriums.
Specimen plant	A plant specifically chosen and cultivated for its exceptional qualities, such as form, color, size, or unique characteristics. Examples are Japanese maple, hydrangea, and hostas.
Stratify	Process of treating seeds to simulate the natural conditions seeds must experience in order for germination to occur to break dormancy.
Suckers	Vigorous roots that grow from the root system or base of a plant rather than from the main stem or branches. Examples include roses and many fruit trees such as apples, cherries, and lemons and are particularly common in grafted trees.
Tuber	Underground storage organ that serves as an energy reservoir for certain plants typically the thickened, fleshy parts of stems or roots. Examples are potatoes, dahlias, and begonias.

References

1. Swan Hose. (n.d.). Container gardening made easy: A beginner's guide to growing plants in small spaces. https://swanhose.com/blogs/general-gardening/container-gardening-made-easy-a-beginner-s-guide-to-growing-plants-in-small-spaces
2. Old Farmer's Almanac. (n.d.). The best gardening tools. https://www.almanac.com/gardening-tools-guide
3. Oregon State University Extension Service. (n.d.). Care and maintenance of garden tools. https://extension.oregonstate.edu/sites/default/files/documents/12281/gardentoolscare.pdf
4. Garden Design. (n.d.). Raised bed gardens. https://www.gardendesign.com/vegetables/raised-beds.html
5. The Spruce. (n.d.). Tips for watering plants growing in containers. https://www.thespruce.com/watering-plants-in-containers-847785
6. University of California Agriculture and Natural Resources. (n.d.). Vegetables - The California Garden Web. https://ucanr.edu
7. University of Minnesota Extension. (n.d.). Yard and garden. https://extension.umn.edu
8. Royal Horticultural Society. (n.d.). https://www.rhs.org.uk
9. University of Alaska Fairbanks. (n.d.). It grows in Alaska. https://itgrowsinalaska.community.uaf.edu
10. Dave's Garden. (n.d.). Plant files. https://davesgarden.com/guides/pf
11. Gardenia. (n.d.). https://www.gardenia.net
12. North American Rock Garden Society. (n.d.). Plant profiles. https://www.nargs.org/plant-profiles
13. Missouri Botanical Garden. (n.d.). Plant finder. https://www.missouribotanicalgarden.org
14. University of Florida IFAS Extension. (n.d.). Gardening solutions – Florida-friendly gardening information. https://ufl.edu
15. YouTube. (n.d.). Beginner raised bed garden mistakes to avoid. https://www.youtube.com
16. YouTube. (n.d.). How to make a simple & cheap raised bed. https://www.youtube.com

17. TMK Home Inspections. (n.d.). 8 flowers and vegetables you can plant in the fall. https://tmkhomeinspections.com/plant-in-the-fall/

18. Old Farmer's Almanac. (n.d.). Companion planting chart and guide for vegetable gardens. https://www.almanac.com/companion-planting-guide-vegetables

19. University of Minnesota Extension. (n.d.). Companion planting in home gardens. https://extension.umn.edu

20. USDA. (2023). USDA plant hardiness zone map. https://planthardiness.ars.usda.gov

21. Old Farmer's Almanac. (n.d.). What planting zone do I live in? Updated USDA plant hardiness map. https://www.almanac.com/what-are-plant-hardiness-zones

22. Gardening Know How. (n.d.). USDA planting zones: What is my growing zone. https://www.gardeningknowhow.com/planting-zones/usda-planting-zone-map.htm

23. Natural Resources Canada. (n.d.). Canada's plant hardiness site. http://planthardiness.gc.ca/?m=1

24. Britannica. (n.d.). Koppen climate classification: Definition, system, & map. https://www.britannica.com

25. Wild Yards. (n.d.). The best soil mixture for raised vegetable garden beds. https://wildyards.com

26. Get Busy Gardening. (n.d.). The best soil for container gardening (with recipe!). https://getbusygardening.com

Made in United States
Troutdale, OR
10/30/2024

24311289R10116